REMEMBERING WHO WE ARE

REMEMBERING WHO WE ARE

★

A TREASURY OF CONSERVATIVE
COMMENCEMENT ADDRESSES

ZEV CHAFETS

Sentinel

SENTINEL
Published by the Penguin Publishing Group
Penguin Random House LLC
375 Hudson Street
New York, New York 10014

USA | Canada | UK | Ireland | Australia | New Zealand | India | South Africa | China
penguin.com
A Penguin Random House Company

First published by Sentinel, an imprint of Penguin Publishing Group, a division of Penguin Random
House LLC, 2015

Acknowledgment is made for permission to publish the selections by the following individuals:

Roger Ailes	Bobby Jindal
Ayaan Hirsi Ali	Rush Limbaugh
Arthur Brooks	David Mamet
Ben Carson	Theodore Olson
Chris Christie	Bill O'Reilly
Ryan Crocker	P. J. O'Rourke
Mary Eberstadt	Thomas Sargent
Carly Fiorina	George Will
Victor Davis Hanson	Juan Williams
Brit Hume	Mortimer Zuckerman

Holy Cross Commencement Speech by Marilynne Robinson. Copyright © 2011 by Marilynne
Robinson. Reprinted by permission of Marilynne Robinson.
"The Real Public Service" by Thomas Sowell. © 1999 creators.com. By permission of Thomas
Sowell and Creators Syndicate, Inc.
"To the class of 2012: Attention graduates: Tone down your egos, shape up your minds" and "To the
class of 2014: Students who demand emotional pampering deserve intellectual derision" by Bret
Stephens. (The two works appear in this volume as "Letters to Graduates"). Reprinted with
permission of The Wall Street Journal. Copyright © 2012, 2014 Dow Jones & Company, Inc. All
rights reserved worldwide. License numbers 3554830084171 and 3554821375186.

ISBN 978-1-59184-818-9

Printed in the United States of America

1   3   5   7   9   10   8   6   4   2

Set in Garamond MT Std • *Designed by Alissa Rose Theodor*

To Victoria Gonzalez-Vega

Contents

Remembering Who We Are

INTRODUCTION

Every spring, thousands of American higher learning institutions and tens of thousands of high schools send their graduates off with a commencement ceremony. A centerpiece of the event, as old as American education itself, is the commencement speech. At their best, these speeches furnish students with wise and inspiring advice for the future. The choice of speaker is also part of the message; it signals the sort of person of whom the university, college, or high school approves.

Michael Bloomberg, the former mayor of New York and the tenth richest person in the country, was Harvard University's choice in 2014. The selection was not entirely disinterested. Bloomberg, a Harvard MBA, is perhaps the largest single educational philanthropist in the country. In the past he had donated $350 million to Harvard (and more than a billion to his undergraduate alma mater, Johns Hopkins). Who knew what flights of largesse might be inspired by an invitation to deliver Harvard's 363rd commencement speech?

But just being rich isn't sufficient for a commencement honor by Harvard or other elite, liberal universities. You must also be politically and culturally simpatico. Bloomberg seemed perfect. A political independent, he supported Barack Obama in 2012, as did virtually everyone at Harvard. He is a leader in progressive social issues such as gun control, immigration reform, climate change, abortion rights, and gay marriage.

The Harvard committee that chose Bloomberg had every reason to expect a warm, congratulatory address to the graduates. But commencement had a different meaning for Bloomberg. He took it as an occasion to accuse the nation's most liberal universities, including his host, of betraying their deepest notional value: tolerance.

"There is an idea floating around college campuses—including here at Harvard—that scholars should be funded only if their work conforms to a particular view of justice," he said. "There's a word for that idea: censorship. And it is just a modern-day form of McCarthyism." Bloomberg cited data from the Federal Election Commission showing that 96 percent of Ivy League faculty and administrators who gave money to a presidential candidate in 2012 donated to Barack Obama.

"There was more disagreement than that among the members of the old Soviet Politburo," he said, adding that "a university cannot be great if its faculty is politically homogenous."

As exhibit A of this campus intolerance, Bloomberg offered the current commencement season. Just a few weeks earlier,

Brandeis University had disinvited human rights activist Ayaan Hirsi Ali from delivering a graduation speech. A Somali Muslim who has lived much of her adult life under death threats because of her critique of Islam's treatment of women and gays, Hirsi Ali seemed a perfect speaker for the liberal university— until a cadre of Muslim activists and radical faculty denounced her. Instead of supporting Hirsi Ali's right to speak, the president of Brandeis caved to the pressure and told her she wouldn't be welcome at commencement due to "certain of her past statements" that were, in his view, inconsistent with the university's "core values." He didn't elaborate on what those values were, but they clearly didn't include intellectual diversity. Compounding the insult, he had the audacity to invite Hirsi Ali to visit the school someday for a discussion "in the spirit of free expression that has defined Brandeis University through its history." Presumably, such a discussion would be vetted first by the Muslim students and radical professors whose protests had made Hirsi Ali persona non grata.

Former secretary of state Condoleezza Rice was invited to give the commencement speech at Rutgers University that spring. Rice, like Hirsi Ali, is a distinguished woman of color who overcame childhood discrimination and bigotry to rise to international prominence.

As Secretary Rice prepared her remarks, campus activists mobilized to keep her off the podium. The leaders of Rutgers's Muslim organizations sent a letter to the school's president, accusing Rice of "grave human rights violations," and denounced her publicly as a "war criminal." Rice had helped lead American wars against Al Qaeda, the Taliban, and the regime of Saddam Hussein. Muslims had died in these wars. This, the protesters asserted, gave them the right to veto Rice's appearance (a precedent, given America's generational struggle against Islamic fundamentalism, that would disqualify senior members of the Obama team and every foreseeable administration). The students also staged demonstrations, occupying a campus building and frightening the school's administration. Rutgers was obviously relieved when Rice, disinclined to face such hostility, offered to cancel. The school's administration made no attempt to dissuade her.

A trend seemed to be developing. Students at Haverford College, an elite Quaker school near Philadelphia, forced the withdrawal of scheduled commencement speaker Robert Birgeneau, former chancellor of the University of California, Berkeley. His crime was calling the cops when Occupy demonstrators set up tents on campus. At Smith College, an elite Massachusetts women's school, a petition was circulated against Christine Lagarde's appearance at commencement. Lagarde, the first female managing director of the International Monetary Fund, was accused of heading an organization that promoted "imperialist and patriarchal systems that oppress and abuse women worldwide," and of failing to stand "in unity with equality for all women regardless of race, ethnicity or class." Five hundred students and faculty signed the petition, a very considerable number on a campus of three thousand. Lagarde did the math and bowed out. She was replaced by Ruth Simmons, former president of Smith College and an Obama appointee to the President's Commission on White House Fellowships.

Bloomberg pointed to these and other recent silencings, such as those of former undersecretary of state Robert Zoellick at Swarthmore and Dr. Benjamin Carson at Johns Hopkins. "In each case liberals silenced a voice—and denied an honorary degree—to individuals they deemed politically objectionable," he said. It was especially outrageous, he added, because these incidents of censorship of dissenting views had taken place at elite schools in the Northeast, "a bastion of self-professed liberal tolerance."

The silencing of invited commencement speakers made news because it was so blatant. But, in fact, commencement speakers at elite universities are almost always right-thinking liberals. In the wake of the recent epidemic of disinvitation, Harry Enten of the Web site FiveThirtyEight took a look at the roster of commencement speakers in the last two years at the nation's top thirty universities and top thirty liberal arts colleges, as ranked by *U.S. News & World Report*. Enten found twenty-five current or past Democratic officeholders and zero for Republicans. (There were two former Republican officeholders, Bloomberg and Chuck Hagel, Obama's former secretary of defense.)

Ostensibly nonpolitical speakers but indubitably liberal cultural figures were also heard on commencement day at elite institutions. They included thought leaders such as *New Yorker* editor and Obama biographer David Remnick, Oprah Winfrey, authors Toni Morrison, Walter Isaacson, and Rita Dove, tennis star and feminist icon Billie Jean King, media mogul Arianna Huffington, NPR host Terry Gross, ex–*New York Times* executive editor Jill Abramson, and singer-activist John Legend. The only obvious political or cultural conservative in the past two years was Cardinal Timothy Dolan, who spoke at Notre Dame. The rest of the orators were celebrities, scientists, scholars, and philanthropists. They weren't ideologically identifiable, but it is a fair guess that none had committed crimes against *bien-pensant* doctrine. We would have certainly heard.

It would be hard to argue that irreparable harm has been done to the graduates exposed to a doctrinal orthodoxy on commencement day. They are, after all, finished products of a liberal education, marinated for four years in academic and social sauce prepared from politically correct ingredients. Those who came to campus as liberals are very likely leaving the same way. Some who arrived as conservatives have seen the light. It is unlikely that the graduates will be lastingly edified by the parting thoughts of Arianna Huffington, John Kerry, or Billie Jean King.

What these elite students lose—throughout their education and, most visibly, on graduation day—is an opportunity to hear speakers who will challenge the conventional wisdom and encourage them to consider the possibility that all the smart, cool, talented, and virtuous role models in the country happen to be mirror images of themselves. This reinforces the self-gratifying notion that the leadership class is blessed with a monopoly on wisdom and talent. This delusion has had lamentable repercussions since the Kennedy administration's "best and brightest" led the country into Vietnam, and it is alive and on display in the persistent pratfalls of the Obama administration.

There is a wide spectrum of conservative thinking in this collection. My purpose is not to develop a right-wing orthodoxy, but precisely to show the intellectual and cultural nuance on that side of the spectrum. And so you find Ben Carson who opposes gay marriage and Ted Olson who advocated for it in California; Bobby Jindal, a devout evangelical, and George Will, a self-described "amiable, low voltage atheist." There are blue state Republicans and red; libertarians and Tea Partiers; fiscal conservatives and big spenders.

Some of the contributors would not call themselves conservatives. But their views—on American exceptionalism, religious traditionalism, party affiliation, foreign affairs, or constitutional government—place them in that camp. They would not all agree with one another on any particular issue. Nor do I. I have included even those with whom I disagree in this anthology for the same reason that elite schools need to include conservatives on their commencement day platforms: because it is literally impossible to maintain an open society without hearing and understanding the other side.

Most of the speeches (or columns, in some cases) in this volume are not explicitly political or programmatic. They were meant to enlighten and inspire. It is my hope that gathering them in a single volume will enlighten liberals by exposing them to new and unconventional thoughts; and will inspire conservatives—especially young conservatives—with the realization that there are plenty of brilliant, talented, and eminent men and women who share their views and who speak to, and for, them.

—Zev Chafets

DON'T WAVER IN
TELLING THE TRUTH

★

ROGER AILES

University of North Carolina School of Journalism
and Mass Communication

CLASS OF 2012

ROGER AILES is the chairman and chief executive of
FOX News. He has also served as a consultant for Presidents
Nixon, Reagan, and George H. W. Bush. Before politics,
he was the executive producer of *The Mike Douglas Show*.

The Mike Douglas Show is one of the early talk shows, and
you used to book anybody who was in town. So, you could
have Dr. Edward Teller and wrestling bears on the same show,
didn't matter because they were both there and you had to put
somebody on. And one day a member of my staff ran up and
said, "Oh, my God." I said what's the problem? They said,

"We've got Richard Nixon coming in the front door," Vice President Nixon, this was 1967, and we have Little Egypt, the belly dancer, in the green room with a boa constrictor.

So, I said, "Look, I don't want to scare him, and I sure as hell don't want to scare that snake. So look, put one of them in my office." So, when I got back to my office, there was Nixon. I got into a bit of a discussion with him about television and losing elections, and somehow he had somebody call me in a couple of days and so I worked in that campaign, not in politics. I was—now, if you read *The New York Times*, I was in charge of politics and the Southern strategy. I was actually in charge of key lights and backlights and cameras. But at any rate, I've always wondered if they had put Little Egypt in my office, would I have had more fun in my career? It's worth considering.

I have a twelve-year-old son now, so I'm very interested in education. We went through the last twenty-five years where they told all the kids they have to all get a trophy. Did you guys go through that? Anyway, there's a whole generation of people who think—or are still waiting for their trophy because they think they won something.

Recently, even at the grade-school level, they're going back to making people actually earn grades. And I'm sure here, you have to earn your grades. So, I think that's gone away, but I do think self-confidence and self-esteem in students is critically important.

One day I was in my son's class, he was about seven, and it was an art class and the teacher was walking all around the room seeing what they were doing. And one little guy was just drawing for all he was worth, and the teacher said, "What are you doing, Bennett?"

He said, "I'm drawing God."

Teacher said, "Well, nobody knows what God looks like."

And he said, "They will in a minute."

I think having self-esteem is really important, but actually being able to do the work is even more important.

First, I want to put a disclaimer here. Anything I say tonight is my fault; I don't speak for News Corporation, I'm not speaking for FOX News, I'm not speaking for Rupert Murdoch. I take full and complete responsibility because nobody else wants it, frankly.

I understand most of you are journalism students. Well, I think you ought to change your major because you're probably all interested in politics and you probably are going into journalism because you think you can affect politics. Well, maybe you can, maybe you can't. But if you're going in to affect it, you have to think about that, because you might want to go to political science where you can join a campaign, help elect who you want, push the issues you believe in. I'm uniquely qualified to talk about that because I did work in politics, made a conscious effort to quit, and did quit, walked away twenty years ago, and now, I run a journalism organization. And people say, "Well, you have no journalism degree, how dare you run a journalism organization? What are your qualifications?"

And as I said to *The New York Times*, I only have two. One, I didn't go to Columbia Journalism School, and two, I never wanted to go to a party in this town anyway, so there's nobody's rear end I have to kiss. If you're going to run a journalism organization, you better be independent. Now, I do guest lectures at many colleges or universities.

I teach occasionally at West Point, or to West Point cadets, so I spend some time, a lot of time, with students. I often ask people why they want to go into journalism. They tell me some version of it's because they want to change the world or save the world. I usually ask them what makes them think the world wants to be changed in the way they want to change it, which stumps them.

The younger journalism students tend to be more progressive. They believe we need to spend more money, taxpayer money, on green energy. Maybe we do, maybe we don't. But that's not their job. The job is to report about green energy, the good, the bad, and the ugly. Up in Ridgewood, New Jersey, they just put solar panels on every telephone pole. Why they want to warm these telephone poles, I don't know. Nobody can figure out. So, we sent a film crew out to interview some of the people, and we said, "Did your energy costs go down?"

They said, "No, they actually went up a little."

And we said, "Well, why did they do this, because they're really ugly?"

And they said, we think it was to count the people who put them on there as green jobs, but don't worry, there's a lot of snow and ice in New Jersey, some will fall and they'll start killing people at bus stops and then they'll come out and take them down.

One-point-five or less percent of our energy today comes from alternative energy. Should we invest? Yes. Should we pretend it's going to solve our problems in the next ten or fifteen years? No. One-point-five percent.

So, that's a way to report that, but you have to report the real numbers and the real facts. If your point of going into journalism is to show how much you care, or how sensitive you are, or to affect the outcome of your personal desires, it's the wrong profession for you. If you want to bring world peace or save starving children, both very noble goals, the way to affect that as a journalist is to investigate why the United Nations is so ineffective at doing either of those, even though they get 22 percent of their budget from the American taxpayers. They seem to have trouble bringing peace, and they seem to have trouble feeding people. We need to question that.

I always tell my journalists, if there's something in your piece that you don't agree with, good. If there's nothing in your piece you don't agree with, you're probably doing a biased job. A nineteenth-century etiquette book said it's improper to kick a newspaperman down the stairs simply because he has chosen to make his living in a disagreeable manner. General Grant wanted all journalists shot as spies. Critics say most injuries to journalists occur by them falling off their egos onto their IQs. I think it's a little rough because many journalists are fine, intelligent people. Hundreds are locked up or killed every year. I've had journalists kidnapped, beaten, it's tough out there. Many are smart, brave, competitive, and believe me, there are easier ways to make a living.

I want to talk a little bit about your course for the future. This is going to set the tone for the rest of your life. I'm currently working on a book about my life, and while I'd like to say to you that it was well planned, my mentor suggested the title be called "Fluke." Not very flattering, but true. As opportunities presented themselves, I figured out how to get it done and I move on. I asked my mentor, "How did I get to be head of a network? How did this happen?"

And he said, "I've known you since you were twenty-two years old," and he said, "I heard the same words over and over and over." I'm going to tell you this because this will make a difference in how you succeed. He said, "Even people who don't like you, Ailes," and there were plenty, he said, "I heard the words 'Get Ailes. Get him because he has ideas. He'll work until everybody else drops. He'll never quit. He'll come up with inventive ideas. And he won't suck the air out of the room while he's doing it.'"

If you're a person and they put your name next to "get," then the chances are, you're going to have a great career.

There are going to be tough times. Thomas More once said, "You must not abandon the ship in a storm because you cannot control the winds." The winds will blow. The change will come. The most important thing for you to learn is you must adapt to the change. Journalism is changing—you change every day. You're on this, you're on that, you've got input, you've got to make a decision, you do this, that. If you're not a person who can change, this is also not the profession for you.

Now, you're going to hear your country criticized. As a journalist, you must question your country. But you must also question the criticism of the country, which is rarely done. We live in a country where we believe individuals are innocent until proven guilty, but often don't give that same time to our country. So, we shouldn't get up every morning saying, "What did our country do wrong?" We should question the country and question the questioning of the country because after 235 years, it's small, it's young, it needs protection. Who better to protect it than the ones who actually enjoy the freedoms provided by this country?

Of course, America can be improved. Of course, we make terrible mistakes from time to time. But in the end, the United States has fed more and freed more people than all of the other countries put together. You must take that into account.

We have a historic, heroic history. Don't let people attack your traditional values if you have them, or your institutions that have been a beacon of light. American exceptionalism does exist because we believe in freedom. And you can tell this is a great country because everybody's trying to get in and nobody's trying to get out.

I just saw a story a few weeks ago on our air and I said, "Oh, this sounds like a really terrible country. Boy, this is awful." So, I called our desk in the newsroom and I said, "Have you got any pictures of the lines?"

And he said, "What lines?"

I said, "Well, God, if I lived in a country like that, they must be lined up to get out of here."

He said, "Nobody's trying to get out."

I said, "My point exactly. Nobody's trying to get out."

Another point. Don't let people talk you out of trying to

succeed or make you feel guilty about making money. We have a responsibility to assist the poor, not just directly through charity, although that is a big responsibility, but by creating jobs and opportunities for them. If you have the ability and the spirit and you can create a business, that's a major contribution to society and a major contribution to poor people. Every major journalism company I know is run by a rich guy, and I like those guys. Every time I needed a job, I had to go to a rich guy. I love the poor guy; he had no job. I got a job. I tried to help the poor, okay? But I'm not going to let anybody divide me against the people who actually gave me the jobs. That does not seem very productive.

Don't be afraid of challenges. Much of your success will come from taking difficult situations head-on. When I started the FOX News Channel, we had six months. We had no studios, no talent, no programming, no news gathering, no shows, no staff, no control rooms, nothing. I was up against Time Warner; they had a seventeen-year head start with CNN. I had to take on Microsoft and GE that owned NBC. They had unlimited resources. They were launching MSNBC in July of '96. I said, "I've got to launch this year against them because if they get too far ahead, we'll never have room for three channels." So, I launched it in six months.

We passed both of those networks and for ten straight years, we've not lost a single day to either one of them. We just completed fifty-eight consecutive quarters of operating profit growth. In fiscal 2012, coming up here in June, we'll probably do $1 billion in profit. The asset value is somewhere between $12 and $13 billion from an empty room in fifteen years.

We've been 123 months through March 12, forty-one quarters of number-one position in cable news, ten and a quarter years. We have six shows that have maintained the number-one position for over one hundred consecutive months. The top ten out of thirteen shows are on the FOX News Channel. In prime time, CNN is number thirty-one, MSNBC is number twenty-three, and FOX News is number four. In total day, we're number five, but MSNBC is number twenty-six and CNN is number thirty-two.

Why is this important? And I'm not bragging. I got one talent. I pick good people. So, I have a staff that really puts it together, makes it work. That's my talent. Picking good people. Although, as some people point out, most of them are blond. It's not true. I asked my assistant that once because she said, "You know, you've been accused of hiring blondes. Your wife's blond. You like blondes."

I said, "Do I hire a lot of blondes?"

She said, "You get most of your on-air talent from tape and 95 percent of the tapes that come in here are blondes because when women get into television, they dye their hair blond."

So, I said, "Oh, that's why we have so many blondes." So, anyway. It's not my fault.

But I tell you about these ratings because ratings bring in money, and that's how you get a paycheck. Oh, my God, a paycheck. You mean we're not doing this for some higher reason? Yes, you are doing it for a higher reason. But without the paycheck, you're not doing it at all. So, we've been able to put food on the table for our employees and we are the only news network that has not had any layoffs because of economic reasons. Why? Because we win. So, winning's not bad, but everybody doesn't get a trophy.

Your generation will determine whether the American way of life can continue. Don't waver in telling the truth and don't fight for a tie. There's a disadvantage to winning. People will criticize you. They will particularly hate you if you beat them. Many of them are just pathetic people who think every kid should get the trophy. Some of them are actually untalented, vicious people who won't be able to stand the fact that you're more talented or work harder than they do and make more money. So, they'll say terrible things about you. You must be able to withstand that.

They will ascribe motives to you that they don't have and they will tell people what you think when they actually have no idea. A few practical pointers in business. The best advice I ever heard was from an old management consultant who died at age ninety-six, Peter Drucker, who said—spent his entire career writing about business and it came down to two words: the difference between activity and results. We're going to have a meeting, we care, we'll postpone, let's have a dialogue about it, please send me a memo, is all activity. When a problem is solved, something is accomplished, that's a result. Don't ever confuse the two.

I have a friend—well, he's sort of an alcoholic, he always knows when it's five o'clock for some reason, but he says, "I have all the money I'm ever going to need as long as I die by four o'clock tomorrow." He's not worried about money. That isn't how he defines success. You have to define it for yourself.

When I was a kid, I thought, "Gee, if I could ever make $20,000, I'd be rich." Now that's well below the poverty line. So, they keep moving the goalpost on you anyway. Don't focus on that. The money will come if you do the right thing and you use your talent well. Secret to jobs is find something you like to do and get somebody to pay you to do it. Then, you're doing what you like and you have the income you need.

I'm not a big fan of government confiscating more than a third of what we make. I think a third's fair. There's a lot of stuff to be paid for. I'm not just a big fan of that. I do believe greatly in giving to charity voluntarily. When I was young, I thought, "I'm never going to be happy until I'm successful," and it took me a long time to figure out I was never going to be successful until I was happy. And so, I turned it around, and I'm having a great time with my kid and I'm happy.

When I was a young man, I talked to someone who was faced with triumph and disaster. His name was Martin Luther King. I was doing *The Mike Douglas Show* and I had three encounters, I would say, with him. And in two of those, he was sent to my office to wait to go on the air and so I had a chance to sit and chat with him. He was a very brave man because he knew that he could die. He was under tremendous pressure to lead a violent revolution and he refused to do it. He said we'd change the country peacefully. He lost his life doing it. But, he's gone down in history as a great man.

Always respect the people who want peace and will risk their own life to get it. If you watch FOX, you know we do a lot with the military because we have a lot of regard for the people who put their lives on the line. They are warriors who don't want war. It's actually not in their best interest or their family's to have war. But they are willing to die for peace if it comes to that. And so, we need to respect that group. That's one of the reasons I go up to West Point, work with them on the media and the military. They've chosen a profession to protect the peace. They defend the Constitution, which was written to protect us from government. That's why it was written. Everybody who wrote it came from countries where the government got a little too oppressive. There's only one job protected in the Constitution, journalists. They actually decided, "We're not going to take cake decorators or doctors, we're going to protect journalists because they are in place to protect us from an oppressive government, from things we don't need or want, from staying in power too long so they can have power."

People who came to this country came from places where the government showed up in the dark of night and took away their family members, took away their possessions, and took away their dignity. The Constitution was written to protect our freedoms: speech, press, freedom to openly practice our religion without the government telling us where or when we can do it. There's nothing in there that says you can't pray in an end zone or a Dairy Queen. It says you really can't interfere with people's right to express their religion at all.

The press was set up to keep an eye on this government. Thomas Jefferson said it, if it were left to me to decide whether we should have a government without newspapers or newspapers without a government, I'd not hesitate for a moment to prefer the latter. So, when the press becomes subservient to the government or falls in love with politicians or neglects their responsibility, journalism has to act as a watchdog, not a lapdog, not an attack dog, but as a watchdog.

While freedom of the press is a central pillar of democracy, freedom of the press did not invent democracy. Democracy is the structure, the support, the cradle for freedom of the press. So, democracy depends on freedom of the press. But freedom depends on fairness in the press. There has to be more than one point of view.

When I started FOX News in '96, I wrote the following mission statement. I wrote it the morning we launched.

"FOX News is committed to providing viewers with more factual information and a balanced and fair presentation. FOX believes viewers should make their own judgment on important issues based on unbiased coverage. Our motto is we report, you decide. Our job is to give the American people information they can use to lead their lives more effectively. And our job is to tell them the truth wherever the truth falls."

Now, I'll tell you something that will surprise you. In fifteen years, we have never taken a story down because we got it wrong. You cannot say that about CBS. You cannot say that about CNN. You cannot say that about *The New York Times*, and the mainstream media won't report it, but that is the fact. We've lived with this bull's-eye on us for fifteen years and our journalism actually is very good. Now, when you watch it, some people say it's too conservative. So, they look at it, they don't understand. We have journalism and you have talk shows, and all cable news—CNN has talk shows, MSNBC has talk shows, Rachel Maddow has a talk show, Sean Hannity has a talk show. That's fine. That's not the actual journalism. Shep Smith, the wheel that runs during the day, the news stories that break, that's the hard journalism. And somebody said to me, "Well, don't you work for that kind of conservative FOX News Channel?"

And I said, "Let me ask you a question. Are you comfortable with CNN?"

They said, "Yes."

I said, "What about MSNBC?"

"Oh, they're great."

"ABC, NBC, CBS okay?"

"Yep, fine."

"PBS? NPR, great?"

"Yep. Great."

"*New York Times, Washington Post, L.A. Times* fine?"

"Great."

So, I said what you're really telling me is that there's a little cable channel over here that's driving you nuts because it won't line up with your worldview. Don't you think it's valuable to have at least one little voice in the wilderness that might differ? I said, "Remember, the last time all of us got lined up together, they lined it by two guys. Hitler and Stalin."

So, if there's an alternative point of view, don't wet your pants. Suck it up and say, "Hey, there's room for everybody."

Now, four things I tell my people, if they want a great career, they have to do these things. If they don't do them, they will fail. One: excellence. Requires hard work, clear thinking, application of your unique talent. A desire to do better every day at your job is the cornerstone of a great career.

Integrity. Nothing is more important than giving your word and keeping it. Don't blame others for their mistakes, don't take credit for other people's work. Don't lie, cheat, or steal; people always figure it out and you never get your reputation back.

Three: teamwork. Our common goal is to win. Teams go to the Super Bowl. Volunteer to help somebody else when your job's finished, ask for help if you need it, solve problems together, give credit to the others, and remember, loyalty is a two-way street. Don't expect it if you don't give it.

And the last is attitude. Attitude is everything. You live in your own mind. If you believe you're a victim, you will be a victim. If you believe you will succeed, you will. Negative people make positive people sick. And all progress depends on positive people. With that last note of attitude and hoping you have a good attitude so you're really nice in your questioning, I'll thank you all for allowing me to speak tonight at this great institution.

What I Would Have Said at Brandeis

AYAAN HIRSI ALI

Published in *The Wall Street Journal*

April 10, 2014

AYAAN HIRSI ALI is a Somali-born activist currently based in America. She is an outspoken critic of radical Islam. The following column was published in April 2014 after her invitation to deliver a commencement address at Brandeis University was rescinded due to protests from Muslim student groups.

One year ago, the city and suburbs of Boston were still in mourning. Families who only weeks earlier had children and siblings to hug were left with only photographs and memories. Still others were hovering over bedsides, watching as young men, women, and children endured painful surgeries and permanent disfiguration. All because two brothers, radicalized by jihadist Web sites, decided to place homemade bombs in backpacks near the finish line of one of the most prominent events in American sports, the Boston Marathon.

All of you in the Class of 2014 will never forget that day and the days that followed. You will never forget when you heard the news, where you were, or what you were doing. And when you return here, ten, fifteen, or twenty-five years from now, you will be reminded of it. The bombs exploded just ten miles from this campus.

I read an article recently that said many adults don't remember much from before the age of eight. That means some of your earliest childhood memories may well be of that September morning simply known as "9/11."

You deserve better memories than 9/11 and the Boston Marathon bombing. And you are not the only ones. In Syria, at least 120,000 people have been killed, not simply in battle, but in wholesale massacres, in a civil war that is increasingly waged across a sectarian divide. Violence is escalating in Iraq, in Lebanon, in Libya, in Egypt. And far more than was the case when you were born, organized violence in the world today is disproportionately concentrated in the Muslim world.

Another striking feature of the countries I have just named, and of the Middle East generally, is that violence against women is also increasing. In Saudi Arabia, there has been a noticeable rise in the practice of female genital mutilation. In Egypt, 99 percent of women report being sexually harassed and up to eighty sexual assaults occur in a single day.

Especially troubling is the way the status of women as

second-class citizens is being cemented in legislation. In Iraq, a law is being proposed that lowers to nine the legal age at which a girl can be forced into marriage. That same law would give a husband the right to deny his wife permission to leave the house.

Sadly, the list could go on. I hope I speak for many when I say that this is not the world that my generation meant to bequeath yours. When you were born, the West was jubilant, having defeated Soviet communism. An international coalition had forced Saddam Hussein out of Kuwait. The next mission for American armed forces would be famine relief in my homeland of Somalia. There was no Department of Homeland Security, and few Americans talked about terrorism.

Two decades ago, not even the bleakest pessimist would have anticipated all that has gone wrong in the part of the world where I grew up. After so many victories for feminism in the West, no one would have predicted that women's basic human rights would actually be reduced in so many countries as the twentieth century gave way to the twenty-first.

Today, however, I am going to predict a better future, because I believe that the pendulum has swung almost as far as it possibly can in the wrong direction.

When I see millions of women in Afghanistan defying threats from the Taliban and lining up to vote; when I see women in Saudi Arabia defying an absurd ban on female driving; and when I see Tunisian women celebrating the conviction of a group of policemen for a heinous gang rape, I feel more optimistic than I did a few years ago. The misnamed Arab Spring has been a revolution full of disappointments. But I believe it has created an opportunity for traditional forms of authority—including patri-archal authority—to be challenged, and even for the religious justifications for the oppression of women to be questioned.

Yet for that opportunity to be fulfilled, we in the West must provide the right kind of encouragement. Just as the city of Boston was once the cradle of a new ideal of liberty, we need to return to our roots by becoming once again a beacon of free thought and civility for the twenty-first century. When there is injustice, we need to speak out, not simply with con-demnation, but with concrete actions.

One of the best places to do that is in our institutions of higher learning. We need to make our universities temples not of dogmatic orthodoxy, but of truly critical thinking, where all ideas are welcome and where civil debate is encouraged. I'm used to being shouted down on campuses, so I am grateful for the opportunity to address you today. I do not expect all of you to agree with me, but I very much appreciate your willingness to listen.

I stand before you as someone who is fighting for women's and girls' basic rights globally. And I stand before you as some-one who is not afraid to ask difficult questions about the role of religion in that fight.

The connection between violence, particularly violence against women, and Islam is too clear to be ignored. We do no favors to students, faculty, nonbelievers, and people of faith when we shut our eyes to this link, when we excuse rather than reflect.

So I ask: Is the concept of holy war compatible with our

ideal of religious toleration? Is it blasphemy—punishable by death—to question the applicability of certain seventh-century doctrines to our own era? Both Christianity and Judaism have had their eras of reform. I would argue that the time has come for a Muslim Reformation.

Is such an argument inadmissible? It surely should not be at a university that was founded in the wake of the Holocaust, at a time when many American universities still imposed quotas on Jews.

The motto of Brandeis University is "Truth even unto its innermost parts." That is my motto too. For it is only through truth, unsparing truth, that your generation can hope to do better than mine in the struggle for peace, freedom, and equality of the sexes.

THE SECRET TO HAPPINESS

ARTHUR BROOKS

Thomas Edison State College

CLASS OF 2013

ARTHUR BROOKS is a social scientist and the president of the think tank the American Enterprise Institute in Washington, D.C. He is noted for his study of Gross National Happiness.

Happiness has traditionally been thought an elusive and evanescent thing. To some, even trying to achieve it is an exercise in futility. As Nathaniel Hawthorne once said, "Happiness is as a butterfly which, when pursued, is always beyond our grasp, but which if you will sit down quietly, may alight upon you."

It turns out that social scientists have caught the butterfly. Over forty years of research, they have found that happiness comes from three sources: genes, events, and values.

Armed with this knowledge and following a few simple

rules, we can improve our lives and build a society that improves the lives of those around us. We can even construct an economic system that fulfills our Founders' promises and empowers all Americans to pursue happiness for themselves.

Some of life's most important elements defy simple measurement: love, faith, loyalty, passion. Happiness sounds like one of these fuzzy, incalculable things—but it isn't. Psychologists and economists have been measuring happiness since at least the early 1970s.

Simply asking people how happy they are yields surprisingly consistent results. Every year for four decades, about a third of Americans have told the General Social Survey (GSS) that they're "very happy," and another half have said they're "pretty happy." Only about 10 to 15 percent say they're "not too happy." Psychologists have used sophisticated techniques to verify these responses, and the simple surveys have proven accurate.

So what sets happy people apart?

The first answer involves our genes. Researchers at the University of Minnesota compiled data on twins born between 1936 and 1955, including some identical twins separated at birth and adopted by separate families. As genetic carbon copies raised in varying environments, these twins can help us disentangle nature from nurture. These data are a social scientist's dream.

The researchers found that about 48 percent of our happiness is genetic. Since I discovered this, I simply blame all my bad moods on my mother. (You can do that, too.)

One innate characteristic correlated with happiness is gender. Consensus long held that women are happier than men, though several new studies contend that the gap is shrinking or may even have disappeared. At the top line, here's what the very latest data show. In survey data from the 2012 GSS, roughly the same proportion of single women and single men are very happy. But married and divorced women are happier than their male counterparts, and widowed women are much happier than widowed men. My wife seemed much less surprised by this last finding than I was.

Political junkies might be interested to learn that the happiest women are conservatives. Forty percent of conservative or very conservative women say they are very happy, making them slightly happier than conservative men (37 percent) and significantly happier than women who are liberal or very liberal (32 percent). The unhappiest group of all are liberal men, only 22 percent of whom consider themselves "very happy."

So about half of our happiness seems hardwired from the day we're born. But what about the rest? What dimensions of our lives determine how happy we are?

It's tempting to assume that enormous, one-time events will bring the happiness we seek. A particular dream job or an Ivy League acceptance letter seems certain to permanently increase our life satisfaction. And sure enough, studies show that isolated events do control a big fraction of our happiness—about 40 percent at any given time. The lesson seems simple: to get happy, chase your grandiose goals. Right?

Wrong. One-off events do govern much of our happiness at a given moment, but the impact of each particular event is surprisingly short-lived. People presume that making a major change—moving to California or getting a big raise—will make them permanently better off. It won't. Huge goals may take years of hard work to meet, and the striving itself may be worthwhile, but the happiness glow they create dissipates after just a few months.

Dozens of studies confirm this, but one personal favorite is the research on lottery winners.

What would you do if you won the jackpot? Some people say they'd travel more; others would buy a bigger house. If you're a man looking to impress a woman, you say you'd start a foundation. Sure you would.

Such daydreaming rarely goes like this: "If I won the lottery, I'd start by buying a bunch of junk I don't really need or want. Next, I'd get myself into an ill-fated romantic relationship with somebody who doesn't love me. Finally, I'd start a nasty alcoholic spiral."

But as we've all heard, that's what often happens. And even for people who don't crash and burn, the future isn't that great. Lottery winners report a big happiness boost at first, but actually end up less able to wring happiness from simple pleasures and ordinary events than nonwinners.

Don't bet your happiness on big events. If you count on the big brass ring to make you happy, you'll only find frustration.

To review: About 48 percent of happiness is determined by our genes. The big shocks we imagine will change things forever account for another 40 percent, but only affect us for a short period of time.

That leaves only about 12 percent within our control. That may not seem like much, but you can own that 12 percent with your life choices. For it turns out there are four basic things in life that bring the most happiness to the most people: faith, family, community, and work.

George Burns once quipped, "Happiness is having a large, loving, caring, close-knit family—in another city." He was half right. Empirical evidence confirms the obvious: family, along with faith and friendships, are major wellsprings of meaning and satisfaction. Few dying patients look back with sadness and regret on their rich community involvement, solid family ties, and quest for enlightenment.

Work, though, seems much less intuitive. Pop culture portrays our jobs as necessary evils we barely endure. Here's a quiz for you: What percentage of Americans are "satisfied" or "completely satisfied" with their jobs? Do you have a number in your head?

The number in your head is wrong. A big majority of Americans like or love their jobs. GSS data show that more than 50 percent of Americans say they are "completely satisfied" or "very satisfied" with their jobs, rising to over 80 percent when we include "somewhat satisfied." Remarkably, this finding holds across income and education levels.

Why? Because in America, flexible labor markets and a culture of dynamism mean we get to choose our work. In plenty of other societies, your family or your government can say, "You! Herd sheep," and it doesn't much matter if you'd prefer to be a postman. But American workers are historically very mobile, and the U.S. economy is famed for its responsiveness to personal preferences. No wonder most of us like our jobs.

I'm a living example of the happiness vocation can bring. When I was nineteen, I dropped out of college and went on the road playing the French horn. . . . After playing chamber music all over the world, I landed in the Barcelona Symphony.

But when I hit my late twenties, I realized it wasn't the life for me. I called my dad back in Seattle. "Dad, I've got big news. I'm quitting music to go back to school!"

"You can't just drop everything," he objected. "It's very irresponsible." "But I'm not happy," I told him.

There was a long pause, and finally he said, "What makes you so special?!"

But I'm really not special. I was lucky—lucky to catch glimpses of my future unhappy self, and lucky to find a road that made me truly happy. I went to school, spent a blissful decade as a university professor, and wound up running a Washington think tank.

Along the way, I learned two things. First, the right kind of work is unbelievably important. Second, this is emphatically not about the money. That's what research shows as well. Most economists who study happiness find that more money makes a truly poor person happier because it relieves considerable pressure from everyday life—getting enough to eat, having a place to live, taking your kid to the doctor. But scholars such as Nobel Prize winner Daniel Kahneman have found that once people reach middle-class levels, big increases in money bring only small increases in happiness.

So relieving poverty brings big happiness, but pay raises per se do not. For most of us, something beyond money connects our happiness to our work. What is it? Let's examine the clues.

First, simply being productive boosts well-being considerably. Even after accounting for government transfers that keep income fairly constant, unemployment proves catastrophic for happiness. Finances aside, joblessness boosts rates of divorce, disease, and suicide.

Second, nearly three quarters of Americans say that even if a financial windfall enabled them to live in luxury for the rest of their lives without working, they still wouldn't quit their jobs. Those with the least education, the lowest incomes, and the least prestigious jobs were actually most likely to say they would keep working, while elites were likelier to say they would take the money and run. We would do well to remember this before scoffing at "dead-end jobs."

Put these clues together, and your brain will conclude what your heart already knew: work brings happiness by marrying our passions to our skills, empowering us to create value in our lives and in the lives of others. Franklin D. Roosevelt had it right: "Happiness is not in the mere possession of money; it lies in the joy of achievement, in the thrill of creative effort."

In other words, the secret to happiness through work is earned success.

This is not just conjecture. Returning to the GSS, we see that Americans who feel "very" or "completely successful" at work are twice as likely to say they are very happy overall as people who only feel "somewhat successful" on the job. And these differences persist after controlling for income and other demographics.

You can measure your earned success in any currency you choose. You can count it in dollars, sure—or in kids taught to read, habitats protected, or souls saved. When I taught graduate students, I noticed that social entrepreneurs who entered the nonprofit sector were some of my happiest graduates. They made less money than their classmates who pursued for-profit careers, but they were no less certain they were earning their success. They just defined that success in nonmonetary terms, delighting in it all the same.

If you can figure out your own project and discover the true currency of the value of your life, then you'll be earning your success. You will have found the secret to happiness through your work.

In truth, there's nothing new about earned success. It's simply another way of explaining what America's Founders meant when they proclaimed in the Declaration of Independence that humans' inalienable rights include "Life, Liberty and the pursuit of Happiness."

This moral covenant links the Founders to each of us today. The right to define what makes each of us happy and work to attain it—to earn our success—is our birthright. And it is our moral duty to pass it on to our children and grandchildren.

Of course, this raises more questions than it answers. What system spawns earned success? What system empowers us to marry our skills with our passions, celebrates hard work and personal responsibility, lets flourishing flow from merit instead of the color of our skin or the place of our birth?

Good news—such a system exists. It's called free enterprise.

More than mere materialism, free enterprise empowers each individual to treat his or her life (the true "enterprise") as a project. It creates more paths than any other system to use our abilities in deeply meaningful ways, whether that entails great wealth or not. Free enterprise lets people decide if we want to be entrepreneurs, teach kids, minister to the poor, play the French horn, or do something else. It doesn't guarantee we'll make a lot of money or even make a go of it, but it does give us the opportunity to try.

But we have a major problem today, one that free enterprise's moral defenders have been far too slow to recognize. Extending the system's blessings to all people requires real opportunity for everyone. And today, opportunity is in peril.

Research from the Federal Reserve Bank of Boston shows that in the early 1980s, 21 percent of Americans in the bottom income quintile would rise to the middle quintile or higher over a ten-year period. By 2005, that percentage has fallen by a third, to 15 percent. And a 2007 Pew Research Center analysis showed that mobility is more than twice as high today in Canada and Scandinavia than here at home.

Clearly, it is not enough to assume that the free enterprise system blesses each of us with equal opportunities. We have an ethical obligation to make sure that this is so.

That means fighting for the policies and culture that will reverse troubling mobility trends. We need schools that serve children's civil rights instead of adults' job security. We need to encourage job creation for the most marginalized instead of destroying opportunities through excessive regulation. We need to declare war on barriers to entrepreneurship all throughout the income distribution, from hedge funds to lawn care. And we need to revive our moral appreciation for the cultural elements of success—especially family, personal responsibility, and honest work.

We also need to clear up common misconceptions about free enterprise. Free enterprise does not mean destroying the social safety net. It means pivoting to programs that focus relentlessly on lifting up the truly poor and vulnerable, and unleashing the prosperity that can sustain these commitments. It doesn't mean reflexively supporting big business, but leveling the playing field so real competition trumps corporate cronyism. It doesn't mean being an "anything goes" libertine, but standing for self-government and self-control.

And it certainly doesn't mean believing that greed or materialism are laudable or even acceptable. It means championing opportunity for everyone.

The secrets to the happiness under our control are simple. Want to be a happier person? Immerse yourself in faith, family, community, and work. And never waste your time chasing anything unearned.

Want to share your happiness with others? Proudly promote the free enterprise system—not as an efficient economic alternative, but as a moral imperative. Fight to make its blessings abundant to all people, especially our most vulnerable brothers and sisters.

These are the secrets to happiness. This is how we can improve our own lives, lift the hearts of those we love, and extend our good fortune to millions more we will never meet.

Some Common Sense

★

BEN CARSON, MD

Regent University

CLASS OF 2014

DR. BEN CARSON is an accomplished neurosurgeon and best-selling author, most recently of *One Nation: What We Can All Do to Save America's Future*. He rose to political prominence following a passionate speech he delivered at the 2013 National Prayer Breakfast. He was portrayed by Cuba Gooding Jr. in the TV movie *Gifted Hands: The Ben Carson Story*.

America, despite all the things that you hear, is still a place of dreams. And I think there was a reason that God gave us the capacity to dream, because sometimes it seems like maybe those things were not going to come to pass. You know, I dreamed of becoming a doctor. Everything that came on the television or radio that had anything to do with medicine, I was right there. You know, *Dr. Kildare*, Dr. Casey, I was right there listening. I even liked going to the doctor's office, so that tells you I was kind of strange as a kid. But I would gladly sacrifice a shot just to be able to be in there, and going to the hospital was the best thing in the world. Because, you know, a lot of people go to the hospital and they're all mad because they have to wait for a long time to see somebody. It didn't bother me at all. I would just sit out in the hallway and just listen to the PA system.

"Dr. Jones, Dr. Jones, to the emergency room. Dr. Johnson, to the clinic." They just sounded so important. And I was thinking one day they'll be saying "Dr. Carson, Dr. Carson." But, of course, we have beepers now so we still don't get to hear it.

But that dream, sometimes, is the only thing to drive you when everything else seems to be falling apart. And sometimes dreams don't lead to good places, though, and I'm sure some of you remember the case of the Bijani twins, the twenty-nine-year-old Iranian women who were joined at the head. Their lifelong dream was to be separated. They scoured the planet looking for a team willing to take on that kind of risk. Everybody agreed there was no better than a fifty-fifty chance they could survive such an operation. When they first contacted me, I told them about Chang and Eng Bunker, the original Siamese twins, who lived to be sixty-three years old and were never separated, but they didn't want to hear about that.

So they kept looking and they found a team in Singapore who was willing to take on the risk. They had separated a set of twins from Nepal, and I was actually involved in that. So the team managed to convince me to come and help them against my better judgment. But I must say that when I met those young women, I was duly impressed, because they were so smart. They were vivacious. They had learned to speak English in only seven months, if you can imagine that. They both had college degrees. They both had law degrees. Only one wanted one, but they both had law degrees. So they had a very good impression of what they were entering in terms of risk, and they said something that really struck me. They said, "Doctor, we would rather die than spend another day stuck together." And that seemed kind of harsh, but then I did something I highly recommend—I put myself in their shoes. I said, "What would it be like to be stuck to somebody 24/7, couldn't get away for one second?" It could be the person you admire most in the world. How long would you like them for? And I began to understand what it is that they were feeling.

Well, that operation proceeded. We were in the third day. We were 90 percent finished. Some people were celebrating. I was not among them, because when we got to the very last part, bleeding began under such pressure it was impossible to stop. You put a clip on it, it'll rupture behind the clip. And they died. So not everything we do is successful. And really, if you look back through the history of surgery, you'll see the same kind of thing. The first kidney transplants? Disastrous. Same thing with hearts, lungs, livers. You would have said, "Why do they even bother?" But information was being gathered. Data was being accumulated. And we learn from those things, and now all of those procedures are done quite routinely and quite safely, and it says a lot about learning from mistakes.

And it's not only in medicine. You know, Thomas Edison said he knew 999 ways a light bulb did not work. And most of you know the cleaning product Formula 409. Why do they call it that? Because the first 408 didn't work. But, you know, you just learn and move forward. And you think of the famous neurosurgeon at Johns Hopkins, many decades ago, Walter Dandy. He was the first one to do all kinds of things, it was just amazing what he was able to do. First one to operate on a posterior fossa. People said that compartment of the head is too small, the tissue will swell, the patient will die. But Dandy operated on someone with a lesion on the posterior fossa. And the tissue did swell, and they did die. And then another, and they died. And another, and they died. The first thirteen all died. I can't even imagine what he said to the fourteenth patient about how the first thirteen did. He probably said nobody's complaining. But the thing is he learned from it, and now we're able to do posterior fossa operations quite routinely and quite safely.

And it says, again, a tremendous amount about failure and learning from failure. And all of you will have setbacks in your life. And you can become depressed about it or you can analyze it and say "What can I learn from this?" And, you know, nations are capable of doing the same thing—learning from those who preceded them, who made very poor choices. And I'm sure some of you have read *The Decline and Fall of the Roman Empire* and saw the kinds of things that they did. And it's almost as if our nation, now, is reading that book and saying, "Okay, this is what they did, let's make sure we do that." You know, we can do better than that, and I'm hoping many of you will move into legislative arenas and will exercise some wisdom and some direction from God to learn from mistakes that have been made in the past so we don't have to do the same silly things and expect a different result, and that is eminently possible.

Before we go on, I need to mention one very important thing, and that is that I am not politically correct. So it is possible I could offend someone, okay? Not intentional. Not intentional. But, unfortunately, people have become so sensitive these days. When I was a kid, there was a saying: "Sticks and stones may break my bones, but names will never hurt me." I don't think they teach that to the kids anymore. Everybody's so sensitive.

And, really, the emphasis needs to be on learning to develop a thicker hide and not to scrutinize every word that someone said to see if, perhaps, you're going to be hurt by it. You know, we're more mature people than that. We can do better than that. And it seems to me like a lot of people came to this country from all over the world because they were trying to escape from places where people told them what they could say and couldn't say and where they could live and what they had to buy. You know, we're better than that, and we need to recognize that there were a lot of people that sacrificed in order to give us freedom of speech and freedom of expression, and we simply should not submit to the PC police who want to take that away from us.

I actually find them pretty amusing, quite frankly, how if you believe in traditional marriage, you're a homophobe. If you believe in the sanctity of life, and you're pro-life, then you're anti-woman. If you disagree with a progressive black person, you're a racist. If you're a black person and you disagree with a black person, you're crazy. I mean, it's just a pretty crazy thing to me. But, you know, the only power these people have is intimidation. And if you don't submit to their intimidation, they have no power over you. And that's what the American People have to realize, because what they've also tried to do is divide everybody up. Any crack, any crevice, drive a wedge into it to create a war. A war on women. Age wars. Income wars. Racial wars. Any kind of war you can have to divide people up.

But, you know, a wise man by the name of Jesus Christ said a house divided against itself cannot stand, and we have to recognize that we, the American People, are not each other's enemies. The enemies are those people who are trying to divide us up, and what we have to do is learn how to identify them and negate their influence while we work together to strengthen our nation and solve our problems. That is up to us, the American People. We can do that. And, interestingly enough, I kind of understood all of that early on. I began to understand that it's actually okay to disagree with people. And because you disagree with someone doesn't make them your enemy. And, in fact, I'm very fond of saying if two people agree about everything, one of them isn't necessary. And I think we're all necessary.

Really what we need to do is start engaging in civil dialogue. Even if you disagree with somebody, talk to them about it. Very frequently you will find that you have a lot more in common than you have that separates you, and this is what many on the left do not want you to understand. That's why Saul Alinsky said in his book, "Never have a conversation with your adversary, because that humanizes them and your job is to demonize them." And that's why you see so much name-calling and demonization. And we need not to fall into that.

What I'm fond of doing, particularly when having a debate with someone who doesn't espouse the Judeo-Christian values I espouse, and they start calling you names and demonizing you, I simply say to them, "Now that you've completed your gratuitous attack, can we get back to the subject matter?" And that really throws them off and knocks them off their heels. You may want to try that when people try to demonize you.

But, you know, there were a lot of problems with me achieving my dream of becoming a physician, not the least of which was the fact that my parents got divorced early on, and that was devastating. And let me just say to the graduates—some of you are married already, and some of you are going to get married—please marry the right person. Please spend some appropriate time analyzing who you're going to marry. And also recognize that when you take two people from different environments, and you put them under the same roof, there is going to be some friction. Sort of like taking two pieces of sandpaper and rubbing them together. A lot of friction, but if you keep rubbing them together, it gets smooth. And you have to stay in there long enough for it to get smooth, and don't adopt the Hollywood model—to have and to hold, until you get irritated with each other. That's not what the intention was when God formed the institution of marriage, and it is something that we should uphold. And he defined marriage, and we have no business trying to redefine it, because he knows better than anybody else what marriage is.

But, you know, my mother was one of twenty-four children and got married at age thirteen. And she and my father moved from rural Tennessee to Detroit, where he was a factory worker.

And years later, she discovered that he was a bigamist, he had another family. I remember when I told that story at graduation at the University of Utah, nobody thought it was that strange. I told you I wasn't politically correct.

Of course, they don't do that in Utah anymore. But they resolved it in a divorce, and we ended up moving to Boston to live with her sister and brother-in-law. Typical tenement, large, multifamily dwelling. Boarded-up windows and doors, sirens, gangs. Both of my older cousins, who we adored, were killed.

Gigantic rats. The first time I saw one, I thought it was a dog. And roaches that were very aggressive. Not only would they crawl on your table, they would crawl in your cereal box, so if you were eating Raisin Bran, you had to know what those brown things were. And when it said "fortified with protein," you had to understand that.

At any rate, while we were there enjoying that environment, my mother was out working extremely hard, two or three jobs at a time, because she didn't want to be on welfare. And, occasionally, she would have to accept food stamps, but she worked very hard not to let that happen. And she never felt sorry for herself, and that was a good thing. The problem was she never felt sorry for us, either, so there was never any excuse we could give her that was good enough. She would always say, "Do you have a brain?" And if the answer was yes, you could have thought your way out of it. And I think that was perhaps the most important thing that she did for us, was not to accept excuses. Because if you don't accept excuses, particularly with young people, that forces them to look for solutions. It forces them to take on responsibility. And, generally speaking, when you look at people who are successful, they're people who accept responsibility and don't make a lot of excuses.

People who do not achieve a lot tend to have a lot of excuses that they make. Sometimes those people even ascend to high offices, but they still have a ton of excuses about everything, and don't become problem solvers. I want to make sure that that does not occur. But the other thing about my mother is she is incredibly thrifty. She saved every dime, every nickel. A car, she would drive it until it could no longer move. And then she would take all those dimes and nickels and quarters and she would buy a new car. And people would say, "How could this woman afford a new car?" It's because of that thrift. And I do believe that if my mother was the secretary of the treasury, we would not be in a deficit situation in this country.

But just learning commonsensical things in terms of how to manage money makes an incredibly big difference. But her goal was to move back to Detroit, and after a few years we were able to do so. I was a fifth-grade student. I was a horrible student, the worst student you've ever seen in your life, and my nickname was Dummy. They always made fun of me. But I did admire the smart kids. I could never figure out how they knew everything. The teacher would ask a question and their hands would go up and I said, "How do they know so much stuff?" They were the same age as I was. But the kind of student that I was reminds me so much of many students I encounter today, and, sadly, many adults that I encounter today, who really are very low on information.

You know, the Founders of this nation said that our system

was based upon a well-informed and educated populace. And they said if we ever become anything other than that, the nature of the nation will change dramatically. Why is that? Because people would no longer have the ability to critically analyze what they were hearing. And under those circumstances, it would be very easy for slick politicians and dishonest news media to manipulate them. The less information one has, the more easy they are to manipulate.

And there was a time when we were not like that, when education was emphasized as one of the most important things a person could have. Alexis de Tocqueville came to America to study this nation because Europeans were fascinated that a fledgling nation, barely fifty years old, was already competing with them on virtually every level. And one of the things he discovered was that anybody finishing the second grade was completely literate. He could find a beaver trapper and the guy could read the newspaper, could tell him how the government worked, could have a sophisticated conversation. Only the aristocracy in Europe were able to do that. And it was the widespread education among common people of this country that had a profound effect.

You sometimes wonder why those early settlers were so successful. How were they able to move from one sea to another against a rugged and hostile terrain? Because they knew how to build roads, structurally sound bridges, containment facilities, dams. They knew how to invent things when a problem came up. They had the can-do attitude, as opposed to the what-can-you-do-for-me attitude. That's what leads to pinnacle status in record time. It's something that we have to bring back to this nation. It will make all the difference in the world in terms of your future. But education is such an important part of the whole equation. What do you know?

And I would ask everybody here—not just the graduates, all the families, faculty, myself, because none of us are excluded from this one very important thing—promise yourself that over the next year, you're going to spend a half an hour a day learning something new. One half hour a day, that's not a big investment. Get an algebra book, a chemistry book, a physics book. Yes, even physics. There's a physics book called *The Science Before Science* by Anthony Rizzi, it's a user-friendly physics book. Civics, geography, world history, American history, Greek history. Half an hour a day for one year. I guarantee you in a year's time, people who haven't seen you in a while will say, "Who are you?" They will not recognize you. You will be so knowledgeable about everything.

And, you know, knowledge is a formidable foe of falsehood and a formidable ally of truth. And if we have a nation armed with knowledge, it will be very difficult for that nation to be deceived. We have to, once again, get back to that point, because that will be the most significant safeguard against the kind of deception that will fundamentally change the United States of America.

Well, that was something that my mother fully understood. And she knew that I was going nowhere because I was such a bad student, and my brother also. And she prayed to God for wisdom. What could she do to get her sons to get the importance of intellectual development? And you know what? God gave her the wisdom, at least in her opinion. My brother and I didn't think it was wise at all. Turning off the TV? What kind of wisdom was that? And making us read two books apiece from the Detroit public libraries and submit to her written book reports, which she couldn't read. But we didn't know that. She'd put checkmarks and highlights and underlines and stuff. And we thought she was reading but she wasn't. And I was outraged. Everybody was outside having a good time, and there I was inside reading books. And her friends would say, "You can't make boys stay inside reading books. They'll grow up and they'll hate you." And I would overhear them and I would say, "Mother, you know they're right." But it didn't matter, we still had to do it.

And people said, "Why did you read the books? Your mother was always out working." She would have known if we didn't read them. And back in those days, you had to do what your parents told you. There was no social psychologist saying let the kids express themselves, so we had to do it. But the interesting thing is, I started reading those books. And, all of a sudden, when the teacher would ask a question and the smart kids would raise their hands, I would know the answer, too. I would say, "I could answer that. I could have raised my hand." That got me excited. My mother didn't have to make me read books, I would read everything I got my hands on. My mother would say, "Benjamin, put the book down and eat your food." It didn't matter. I was always reading. But in the space of a year and a half, I went from the bottom of the class to the top of the class, much to the consternation of all the kids who used to laugh and call me Dummy.

The same students were now coming to me saying, "Benny, Benny, Benny, how do you work this problem?" And I'd say, "Sit at my feet, youngster, while I instruct you." I was, perhaps, a little obnoxious, but it sure felt good to say that to those turkeys.

The Lord has endowed us all with these tremendous brains. And we are made in the image of God, and God is no dummy. And your brain has billions and billions of neurons, hundreds of billions of connections. It remembers everything you've ever heard, everything you've ever seen. It can process more than two million bits of information per second. You can't overload it. Don't listen to people who say, "Don't learn this, you'll overload your brain," you can't do it! You can learn a new fact every second. It would take you more than three million years to challenge the capacity of your brain. So never worry about that. God has given you everything you need in terms of brain capacity.

And what does he expect of us? He expects us to use that brain to analyze problems, to fix things. You know, we're living in a country right now that has a seventeen-and-a-half-trillion-dollar national debt. That is such a staggering number, it is hard to comprehend. But if you tried to pay it back, at a rate of ten million dollars a day, seven days a week, three hundred and sixty-five days a year, it would take you forty-seven hundred years to pay that back. That gives you some idea of what's happening. The only reason we can sustain a debt like that is because our dollar is a reserve currency of the world.

Can you imagine what happens if it no longer were? And there are a number of nations right now who are talking about that very thing. They want to have a reserve currency that is a composite of many currencies and not just the USA, because they say the USA is fiscally irresponsible. What happens if China, one day, says, "The United States owes us all this money, and they're printing money, and they're devaluating money so the amount they have to pay us back is less. You know what? We're not going to deal with them anymore. We're no longer going to use them as our reserve currency. We're no longer going to buy their treasury securities." And then other nations say, "You know what? That's a good idea, because they make a good point."

And in the world we live in now, in the Internet world, when financial things can change overnight, just ask Lehman Brothers, we can very quickly become a third world nation with the level of debt that we have. And what is necessary is that we, the American People, have to understand this because we're the ones who have to change it. How do we change it? Well, in the early days of this nation, prerevolutionary days, your ancestors were not very happy with what was going on. And they would get together in their communities, in their barns, and they would talk about what kind of nation do we want to have? And they encouraged each other. And that's how a bunch of ragtag militiamen was able to defeat the most powerful empire on earth. It was encouraging each other and talking to each other and deciding what they wanted. This is what we must do again in this nation. We have to start getting together and talking.

You need to start talking to your eighty-seven-year-old aunt, or your eighty-seven-year-old sister, who hasn't voted in twenty years, who might be an invalid, talk to them about what's going on. Help them get an absentee ballot if it's necessary. If they're partially blind, help them fill it out. We have to bring all those people back into the system. Tens of millions of people didn't vote in the last presidential election. We cannot allow that to happen once again. It's up to us, the people. We have to know what we're doing. When we go to vote, we can't just look for a *D* or an *R* or a name that looks familiar, which is what many people do. "Oh, that name looks familiar." The name could be Satan. In many cases, it is. And people just say, "Yeah, that's who I'm voting for." Well, we also have to know how did the people who represent you vote? And if they voted to give away your rights, to create an ever-expanding government, and if they keep voting to raise the debt ceiling, to create an unsustainable debt that will eventually destroy our nation, you need to vote them out of office. That's why the people are at the pinnacle of the system.

But the people have to understand, they have to have knowledge and understanding, in order to exercise that right in the correct way. And then it requires enormous courage, and that's the point I want to finish up on. Enormous courage. Think about the people who made this land of freedom available to us. And think of the courage they had. Think of Nathan Hale, a young rebel caught by the British. Ready to be executed, he said, "My only regret is I have but one life to give for my nation." Two hundred and thirty-nine years ago, Patrick Henry said, "Give me liberty or give me death." George Washington rode with his men. Didn't wait for a report. Incredibly brave. And think about all the things that he talked about in the letter that he wrote.

You know, the people who rewrite our history try to say that our founding fathers were deist, that they didn't have any relationship with God. All you have to do is read the letters that they wrote and you will see that is not true. They had a deep and abiding faith in God. And that's why it's so important when you're doing that half hour of reading, read about that stuff. And read stuff that's contrary to the United States. Read the writings of Karl Marx and Vladimir Lenin and Saul Alinsky and you will see exactly what's happening in our nation today as there are forces that are trying to destroy our Judeo-Christian heritage and our beliefs and put them off to the side and replace them with the very things God says are not right.

But you won't know that unless you read that material and understand the forces against which we are fighting. And I strongly believe from what I've seen around the country, red states, blue states, north, south, east, west, enormous crowds of people [are] very enthusiastic because they want to hear some common sense. And I think this nation is actually in the process of waking up, and I predict that, in November, there will be a big change in the Senate, but that will only be the start. And people have to start thinking about what do we do to change this nation. And when I say "we," I'm not talking about any particular party, I'm talking about people with common sense. People with common sense must, once again, gain control. And when they do, it is very important to govern for all the people and not for just one party, not just for one group of constituents, not to listen to special interest groups because the most important special interest group is the American People. And we have to understand the Constitution and put that foremost, once again, and bring that relationship with God back to the forefront.

And think about World War II. D-Day. Our troops storming the beaches of Normandy, being mowed down by the thousands by the machine gun fire. Did they turn back? No. Did they know they were going to be killed? In many cases, yes. But they stepped over the bodies of their dead comrades, and they overwhelmed the Axis forces. And why did they do it? Because they were concerned about your future and what would happen to you. And, during World War II, as the nations were falling like dominoes before tyrannical forces, the whole world had come under subjugation and only one thing stopped them. This nation. The United States of America, a nation with its ability to send young men from the cities to suburbs to the country to fight a war on two fronts of the world. A nation that had the ability to send its young women into the factories to build more airplanes and mortars than anybody imagined. A nation that, through its determination and its courage and its might, managed to change the course of the world. Those are people who fought for you. When people tell you we are not an exceptional nation, you tell them that story. We are an exceptional nation, and we will become an even more exceptional nation because of the courage that you have. And when you sing the national anthem, the next time you get to the end of that first stanza, and it says "the land of the free and the home of the brave," don't just allow those words to roll off your tongue, but remember that it is impossible to be free if you're not brave. Thank you very much, and thank you for what you're going to do for our nation.

WHAT ARE YOU WILLING TO DO?

⭐

CHRIS CHRISTIE

Rowan University

CLASS OF 2014

CHRIS CHRISTIE is the current governor of New Jersey. Previously, he served as the U.S. attorney for New Jersey and as a county legislator in Morris County. He is chairman of the Republican Governors Association, and was the keynote speaker at the 2012 Republican National Convention.

Education can be a great equalizer. It can make opportunity possible for you no matter where you're from, no matter where your family is from, no matter where you began economically. It can make a difference in your life, it can open doors.

It's also a responsibility. It's a gift that you've been given that gives you a responsibility to use it in a way that helps to better not just your own lives and the lives of your family, but, I think, to better the lives of the places you choose to live over the course of your life. But it's not a guarantee of anything. We've seen many people over the course of our country's history, some with extraordinary education who didn't use it in a way that bettered their lives or the lives of others, and we've seen others with little or no education who have changed our country's history completely. So, today, what you are receiving in that opportunity is something that sets the stage. Gives you the moment, now, to decide what your life will be.

I believe, in the end, what will determine your success or your failure will be how hard you're willing to work. In the end, I think that's the determining factor in most success or failure in life. How you get out of bed every morning, what you see when you look in the mirror, and then what you're willing to do once you walk out the door. Are you willing to give it your all? And if you do, will you really make a difference in your life and the lives of others?

I can cite lots of examples for you of why how hard you work will be the determining factor. I am sure you already have many examples of those in your life. I'll give you the example of one person. This was a person who came to the United States on a boat from Sicily, and who was actually born on that boat between Sicily and the United States. A person who came here, a young woman, growing up in Newark, New Jersey, who, because of the circumstances and the way our society and her culture operated at that time, at a very young age was put into an arranged marriage, something that we can't even conceive of today. Her parents selected her husband for her based on their appreciation for the family he came from.

She entered that arranged marriage and soon had three children. But by the time her first daughter turned ten years old in 1942, she became aware of the fact that her husband was being unfaithful. Now, at that time, in that culture, that was something that women were expected to accept. But this woman had absolutely no intention of accepting that. In fact, she did the exact opposite. She kicked him out of the house and filed for divorce. In 1942. This was simply not done back then very often. She was thirty-three years old, she had no education at all past middle school, and she now had three children to raise on her own because the family she had been arranged into said it was a disgrace that she filed for divorce and there were no laws at that time forcing them or her husband to support her and their children.

And so what did she do? She went out and she looked for a job. And she got a job at the Internal Revenue Service in Bloomfield, New Jersey. She didn't know how to drive, didn't have a driver's license, couldn't afford to buy a car. So she took three buses every morning, beginning at six a.m. to arrive at work by eight a.m. Her ten-year-old daughter was in charge of her seven-year-old sister and her four-year-old brother, to make sure they got to school and day care with lunches and then pick them up after school, because this woman wouldn't arrive home until seven p.m. Every year, at Christmas, they rewrapped the gift they had gotten the year before. And that's what they were given for Christmas because they had no money. Many nights they went to bed hungry, but no nights did they go to bed alone. They had each other. This woman worked without a support system, except for her own belief in herself and her own belief in the fact that her pride, her independence, and her knowledge of who she saw in the mirror was more important than anything else. And she worked for the rest of her life to do that.

That woman became my grandmother. And, as I grew up, I became closer to her than I was to any person in the world. I went to visit her two weekends a month and stay at her apartment. And there were a number of rules that went along with that. On Saturday mornings when we would leave, when I would leave my home and go to hers, the first thing we'd do was walk to the library, where she would return the three books she had borrowed the Saturday before, having read all three of them, and get three new ones. And I would have to get one for myself. I wasn't allowed to watch television, except for two things—and this has led to two of my great obsessions in life, I guess—I was allowed to watch one college football game on Saturday afternoon, and I was allowed to watch *Meet the Press* on Sunday. At eight years old.

She taught me that your life is not determined by what you don't have, but by what you are willing to do. She never remarried, yet she had a full life. She worked all these years at a government job, yet found ways to save money where she traveled the world. We used to travel, once a month, into New York City and she would take me to things I had absolutely no interest in. We'd go to museums that I was bored by. She took me to the opera. Imagine me at the opera. Even then, it seemed incredible.

We went to mass every Sunday morning, and she continued to remind me about just what the president said—how lucky I was to have the opportunities that she saw in front of me.

Every week, until I turned about fifteen, I thought about going, and every other week I did. And the thing that I learned from her, most important, was that her life was full despite all of its challenges, because of the experiences she had, and how hard she worked to get those experiences. You wouldn't have looked at her and thought she would have had a successful life given where she began. But she lived to the age of ninety-two. And she saw her grandson appointed U.S. attorney for New Jersey, weeks before she passed away. And I remember sitting with her, as she was suffering and getting ready to pass, just as I'd been appointed by the president of the United States to be a United States attorney. And she said to me, "Can you imagine how I feel that my grandson—I was born on a boat coming over here, no education, nothing but my own hard work and what I was able to create for myself through the grace of this country—and now you're being appointed to something by the president of the United States." She looked at me and said, "My life is full." Her life was full because her hard work was an example, both to me and to everyone she came in contact with. She never complained about the challenges and she always talked about the opportunities. It's a great lesson for all of us who have been given so much more than that.

We tend, these days, to focus on the negative. We tend to complain about what we don't have, or what hasn't been provided to us. We daydream about all the things that we might be without often thinking about how available it is to us because of the things we've already been given. I learned from my grandmother. She laid that foundation for me. And she taught me that hard work is the key to every success in your life. Whether it's hard work at your career, hard work at your studies, hard work at your marriage, hard work as a parent, there is joy in hard work. You have a leg up, that you've earned today. And that leg up is the education that you've gotten here at Rowan. And now it truly is up to you. And because of the education you have, no one will presume that there are any limits to your life. You will determine, and you alone will determine, the limits to your life. And I believe it will be only determined by your willingness to dream, and, most important, how hard you're willing to work to get there.

In the year that would have been my grandmother's one hundredth birthday, I was elected governor of New Jersey. And I thought often during that campaign—her birthday was September 10th. And I thought often from that day forward to Election Day how amazed she would have been to see what was happening and what might happen. And the day after the election, one of the places that I went to visit was her burial site. I went there just as a sign of respect, to let her know that I understood that I would not have been there without the example she set for me.

I'm not unique. I'm sure for almost every person in this audience, you have someone like my grandmother in your life. Don't believe that the only people who can set examples for you and help you to get where you want to get to are the obvious choices.

Sometimes they're the people with the greatest challenges, who've worked hard, achieved much in their own personal lives, that set an example for you for everything that you could be. Even if what you will achieve in material gain and public notoriety will be well beyond anything they achieved in their lives, or, quite frankly, anything they could have dreamed was realistic for you. I know. I know, today, that my grandmother looks down and shakes her head—often, probably—at some of the things that come out of my mouth and some of the extraordinary opportunities that life has already presented to me.

All of you, I hope both in your hearts and in your spirit, understand that today is just the opening of that door to extraordinary opportunity. And I hope that you know that the people here with you today, myself included, believe in the infinite possibilities for what you can make your life become over the course of the next decades. Believe in yourself as much as those around you believe in you, work as hard as you can, and because of everything else you've achieved here, I believe you, too, will experience a great American life—just like my grandmother did, just like I have. Although very different, they're both great American lives. And you will now write your story. Write it with hard work, write it with belief in yourself, write it with the knowledge that every morning, when you get up, you have the possibility to do something really, really special. Do that. And then, at the end of your life, I think you'll feel the same way that my grandmother felt about hers. "My life is full."

A BALANCED LIFE

★

FRANCIS COLLINS

University of Virginia

Class of 2001

DR. FRANCIS COLLINS is the director of the
National Institutes of Health and the former leader of the
Human Genome Project. He is the author of *The Language of
God: A Scientist Presents Evidence for Belief,* and was appointed
by Pope Benedict XVI to the Pontifical Academy of
Sciences. Collins is also the founder of the BioLogos
Foundation, which serves to advocate the relationship
between science and Christianity.

I have actually tried to remember the dozen or so commencement addresses that I have sat through. And I regret to
say that only one of them leaves the faintest memory of what
was said. But that one, which was actually my high school
graduation, still stays with me to this day. So, with gratitude
and apologies to the Presbyterian minister who delivered it, I
am going to adopt his theme.

This speech consists of an exhortation, supported by a focus on four decisions that I would like you to think about.

The exhortation: Seek a balanced life. Sounds good, but what does that mean? I suggest that this could perhaps be achieved by arriving at satisfactory conclusions to four life decisions. You can think of these as the four food groups of a balanced life, if you wish.

Decision number one: What will be your life's work? Put another way, what will you contribute? What will you leave behind? It has been said that the purpose of life is a life of purpose. What will be yours?

Here on graduation day, many of you already have a clear picture of this. Many of you don't. That is okay. Some of you think you do. And five years from now, you will have completely revised it.

Sitting in your seat thirty-one years ago, I was sure I knew what I wanted to do. I wanted to be a physical scientist working in quantum mechanics. And I went off to get a graduate degree in physical chemistry at Yale. But along the way I discovered molecular biology. Something that I wasn't that aware of because it was just beginning to spring out of the research and biology of the previous few years. And discovering that it was headed for a genuine revolution that would have profound consequences for our understanding of ourselves, I changed fields. I went to medical school and found my passion in medical genetics. A field which as I was here as an undergraduate, I didn't even know existed. So, keep loose. You can't be confident that your plans will be quite as linear as perhaps they seem today. But that is a wonderful privilege to have the chance to make those changes when they come along.

I now have this remarkable job of standing at the helm of the Human Genome Project: this effort, an international effort, to map and sequence all of the letters of our own DNA code, to read our own instruction book. And what an instruction book it is. Inside each cell of your body you have 3.1 billion letters of this DNA code. If I decided because it would make a nice commencement speech to read them for you, and I would read at an average pace of "a, c, g, g, t, a, c, c, g, t, a, c, c . . ." and asked you to stay here because it is such an important day and this is such an important reading, I hope you would have brought along a little refreshment because we would be here for thirty-two years. And you have all that information inside each cell of your body. And guess what, 95 percent of that is now on the Internet for you to go and look at, and try to help us figure out what it means. Because just in the space of the last year, we have crossed a threshold that is of historic significance in our history as the human race. We now have read our own instruction book.

That was done by a cohort of sixteen centers in six countries that I have had the privilege to lead. And it has been an extremely exhilarating experience. In no small part because it involved physics, chemistry, biology, ethics, and theology and a whole host of other disciplines. Would I have predicted that when I sat in your seat? No, and the same will happen to you.

I also find I spend a lot of my time worrying about the ethical implications of this. Will, for instance, if you decide to find out what you are at risk for (because we can now read your DNA sequence) . . . will that information be used to take away your health care or your jobs? That is unjust. That is something that we should put a stop to, but that requires the legislative process to kick in.

When I go to Congress to talk about that, I find myself quoting Thomas Jefferson, who said, "Our laws and institutions must go hand in hand with the progress of the human mind." Yet rapid advances in medical technology of this sort must not be allowed to displace the human touch of medicine. Albert Schweitzer said, "Our technology must never exceed our humanity." We must not forget in these exhilarating days, where so many unknowns become knowns, that the way we touch lives is one at a time. I tend to forget that sometimes. I get carried away with the excitement of the moment.

It always helps me to go back to a day about ten years ago when I spent three weeks working in a missionary hospital in West Africa. If you have not been to the third world, I strongly encourage you to do so. It will change your life.

I went there with my medical student daughter. I had grand ideals about how, in those three weeks, I was going to change the course of health care in Nigeria and those 93 million people who live there would never be the same because I had been there for my three weeks. And I got there working in this very crowded little hospital, surrounded by people with terrible illnesses. I began to feel pretty discouraged. Because while I could help one or two of them, I knew they would go back out to the same environment. And the same conditions that caused them to be ill would still be there.

I was feeling pretty low about this and wondering, "Why am I here?" On rounds one morning, a young farmer who had been admitted almost dead the night before with fluid around his heart from tuberculosis that we were able to draw off and bring him back to at least temporary health—he stopped me and said, "You know, you are different. I have the sense that you haven't been around here very much. And I have a sense that you are wondering why you are here at all." I was a little taken aback. I didn't know it was quite that obvious. And he said, "I want to tell you something. You came here for one reason. You came here for me."

It occurred to me that that is all it ever is about. To reach out to one person, to make a difference in one life, that is really what we are here for. So, have your grand dreams. Have your great plans for what your professional life will be, but don't forget that it is one person at a time where we really leave a legacy.

Decision number two: Well, this is the one that makes people squirm. What are you going to do about faith? Uh oh, not that one. But can there be any more important questions than these: How did we all get here? What is the meaning of life? How is it that we know deep down inside what is right and wrong and yet rarely succeed in doing what is right for more than about thirty minutes? What happens to us after we die?

Surely these are among the most critical questions in life. And ones which a university should carefully consider. But how much time have you spent on them? Perhaps you, like me, grew up in a home where faith played a significant role, but you never made it your own. Or you concluded it was a fuzzy area that made you uncomfortable. Or even concluded that it was all superstition, like Mark Twain's schoolboy, who when requested to define faith said,

"It is believing what you know ain't so." Or perhaps you simply assumed that as you grew in knowledge of science that faith was incompatible with a rigorous intellect and that God was irrelevant and obsolete. Well, I am here to tell you that this is not so.

All of those half-truths against the possibility of God have holes in them big enough to drive a truck through, as I learned by reading C. S. Lewis. In my view, there is no conflict between being a "rigorous, show me the data" physician-scientist and a person who believes in a God who takes a personal interest in each one of us and whose domain is in the spiritual world. A domain not possible to explore by the tools and language of science, but with the heart, the mind, and the soul.

Yet, it is remarkable how many of us fail to consider those questions of eternal significance until some personal crisis or advancing age forces us to face our own spiritual impoverishment. Don't make that mistake.

Decision number three: What are you going to do about love? Well, first love for another. Listen to Jefferson's words, "Nature implanted in our breasts a love of others. A sense of duty to them. A moral instinct, in short, which prompts us irresistibly to feel and suffer their distresses. The creator would indeed have been a bungling artist had he intended man for a social animal without planting in him social dispositions." Listen to those dispositions. Act on them, to all your brothers and sisters.

Sadly, prejudice still abounds in our society. Though genetics is teaching us that there is no scientific basis for drawing sharp boundaries around ethnic or racial groups, we still focus on physical differences of skin color, facial features, and hair texture.

As if they meant something biologically profound. They do not. At the DNA level, we are all 99.9 percent the same. All of us.

And what of romantic love? That enduring, glowing fire! I don't agree with the wag who wrote, "The trouble with loving is that pets don't last long enough and people last too long." Yet our fast-paced and material world places romantic love at risk all too often. So, whether you have found your life's partner or are still looking, make this a priority of the highest order.

So, these three decisions so far: work, faith, and love. What of the fourth one? Well, maybe it doesn't quite belong on the same plane, but I think it is important too.

Decision number four: How will you keep fun in your life? Yes, fun. Seems to be a resonant chord here this morning. Life is full of enough sobering and tragic moments, don't forget to exercise your sense of humor, you are going to need it. Listen to Winston Churchill, "You cannot deal with the most serious things in the world unless you also understand the most amusing."

Now, I admit, fun is a difficult subject to lecture on. So, with apologies to President Casteen for springing this on him, I would like to conclude with a tongue-in-cheek exhibit. A song actually about the university experience, adapted from a little-noticed group from the 1980s, Bright Morning Star. The first two verses of this song are for you, the last is mine. Instrument please.

So, congratulations and Godspeed, Class of 2001. We'll send you off with a little music:

I came, I bought the books, I stayed in the dorms, followed directions.
I worked, I studied hard, made lots of friends that had connections.

I crammed, they gave me grades, and may I say, not in a fair way.
But, I am a good Wahoo, I did it their way.
I learned so many things, although I know I'll never use them.
The courses that I took were all required. I didn't choose them.
You'll find that to survive, it is best to play the doctrinaire way.
And so, I knuckled down, and did it their way.
Well, yes there were times I wondered why
I had to cringe when I could fly
I had my doubts, but after all,
I clipped my wings and learned to crawl.
I learned to bend and in the end, I did it their way.
Not yet . . .

Now, this is my verse:

And now, my fine young friends,
Now that I am a full professor, where once I was oppressed,
I have become the cruel oppressor.
With me, I hope you will see the double helix
Is a highway and yes, you will learn it is best
To do it my way.
Well, wait, wait, wait. . . .
Well, I am just a man, what can I do.
Open your books, read chapter two.
And if it seems a bit routine,
Don't talk to me, go see the Dean.
Just start today, dear UVA,
And do it my way.

Move to the Sound
of the Guns

★

RYAN CROCKER

Whitman College

Class of 2009

RYAN CROCKER was the U.S. ambassador to a
number of Middle Eastern nations. During the period after
9/11 he served in Iraq and Afghanistan and was one of the
key figures in shaping and executing American policy.

Thirty-eight years ago, I sat where you sit. Today I thought
I might offer just a few thoughts on how you could spend the
years that will intervene before you get to stand where I stand.

Lessons from a Long War. At one level, this is America's
campaigns in the world since 9/11 and before. But it is also, I
hope, a campaign each of you will pursue individually as you go
forward, as you seek causes larger and greater than yourselves. I
chose a hard service when I left Whitman. I've never regretted it.

For America and Americans, as the first decade of the twenty-first century draws to a close, there is an ever-greater need to understand the world as it is, not as we may want it to be. It is not a unipolar world, as our adversaries assert and we ourselves may once have hoped. It's a nonpolar world. A world in which we may be the dominant element, but we are by no means the determinative one.

The Cold War, for all of its terrors, provided a stable framework for the post–World War II international order. That framework collapsed with the Soviet Union twenty years ago, and with it, a new disorder was born. It is no coincidence that Iraq, no longer checked by Moscow, invaded Kuwait in 1990. It is therefore a world that must be understood in its own messy, complicated terms, where local and regional realities are always ready to ambush the most sophisticated international strategies. It's a world in which there are few easy choices. In Iraq, we tend to forget the unprecedented challenge that Saddam Hussein posed to the integrity of the United Nations system itself. And if we were wrong, to move without many of our traditional allies, perhaps they were wrong to give us little option except to do so. And maybe, just maybe, we both learned something.

And it is a long war. It started for me, not on 9/11 and in its aftermath, but in Beirut, more than a quarter of a century ago, when the embassy and Marine barracks were bombed. And if it is a long war, it follows that there are real enemies, whether personally or nationally, not all the world wishes us well, and some fights have to be fought. The challenge, the challenge you will face, is knowing which ones, when, and how. It is therefore essential to know our adversaries, as well as our allies. They know us. And with that knowledge, including studies of politics, of history, of culture, and especially of language, to be ready to ask the hard questions. What happens the day, the month, the year after, in a region and in a world where our adversaries may not even start to fight until after we think we have won. But when we are committed, we need to stay committed. Both our allies and our adversaries have drawn dangerous conclusions over the years concerning our commitment and our consistency.

In 2002, America voted for a war in Iraq. In 2006, America voted against that war. But you can't rewind the film. The going has been very difficult, and when I arrived in Baghdad in early 2007 it was somewhere beyond difficult. But sometimes in life, you just have to put your head down and push on. And here's a lesson from a long war: Perseverance does not always require hope, but it can create hope. And both perseverance and hope require a sense of strategic patience. It wasn't only Marcus Whitman's plans that required time and distance. It's America's plans.

So that's a couple of my lessons from a long war in hard places. And whether you know it or not, Class of 2009, you've already gone a long way toward absorbing these lessons, thanks to your education here at Whitman.

President Bridges made a comment to me last night about you as a graduating class: "You know as you graduate, that you don't have all the answers, but you've learned here how to question." You have a much broader global focus than we did when I was here. At least half of you have lived and studied abroad. And the faculty's new global studies initiative promises to take this college to a new level in international affairs.

Now I know that most of you will not specialize in the international arena, but all of you will be informed and affected by it. Wherever and however you engage, I commend to you the most important lesson I have taken out of this long war. It's simple: Be in it. Move to the sound of the guns. Show up for the fight.

I hope some of you will take that literally. Today Americans are fighting and dying for this country. Americans are at war. Tomorrow, we observe Memorial Day. And I hope that all of you, Class of 2009, this entire audience, will take a moment to observe that day as more than just the unofficial beginning of summer.

I hope that all of you in the Class of 2009 will seek service that counts. Believe me, you do not want to be here years from now, counting the sidelines you've stood on, or even just the money you may have made. I hope you will find your own ways and your own wars. There are a lot of them out there.

I was in Montgomery, Alabama, last week, and I had the opportunity to visit the Southern Poverty Law Center, where I was reminded that the struggle for civil rights and against hatred in America is by no means over. Nor is it exclusively a Southern problem.

The Center and its courageous staff came up here, to this area, to take on the Aryan Nation just up the road. And they effectively sued them out of existence. It is a reminder that in life, you get what is just, often, only if you are ready to fight for it. And this, ladies and gentlemen, is a fight; it's an American fight, very much worth being in. . . .

Seniors, enjoy the day. This is commencement. Reality begins on Tuesday. Be on time. And move to the sound of the guns.

The Miracle of Freedom

★

TED CRUZ

Hillsdale College, originally printed in *Imprimis*

Class of 2013

TED CRUZ is the junior U.S. senator from Texas. He has served as director of the Office of Policy Planning at the Federal Trade Commission, an associate deputy attorney general at the U.S. Department of Justice, and a domestic policy adviser to George W. Bush during the 2000 presidential campaign.

This morning I had the opportunity to tour your wonderful campus, and one of the highlights for me was the statue of Margaret Thatcher. I understand that when the statue was unveiled, she sent a letter of praise that read: "Hillsdale College symbolizes everything that is good and true in America. You uphold the principles and cherish the values which have made your country a beacon of hope." I couldn't agree more. There are commencements being held on campuses all over the country this spring, but this one is different. Hillsdale, it is known across the country, is in a class by itself. Those graduating from other colleges are being told to go out and make something of themselves. But for the men and women receiving their degrees here today, expectations are higher. Because of the education you received here, you are uniquely prepared to provide desperately needed, principled leadership to your families, your churches, your communities, your country, and your fellow man. While other graduates have been exposed to college courses such as "Lady Gaga and the Sociology of Fame," you have been grounded in an understanding of our Constitution and of the freedom it was designed to preserve.

Last month the world lost Baroness Thatcher, and in her honor I'd like to spend a few minutes discussing with you the miracle of freedom.

In the history of mankind, freedom has been the exception. Governed by kings and queens, human beings were told that power starts at the top and flows down; that their rights emanate from a monarch and may be taken away at the monarch's whim. The British began a revolution against this way of thinking in a meadow called Runnymede in 1215. It was embodied in the Magna Carta, which read: "To all free men of our kingdom we have also granted, for us and our heirs forever, all the liberties written out below, to have and to keep for them and their heirs. . . ." That revolution reached full flower in Philadelphia in 1787, in a Constitution that began from two radical premises. The first is that our rights come not from kings or queens—or even from presidents—but from God. As the

Declaration of Independence put it, "We hold these truths to be self-evident, that all men are created equal, that they are endowed by their Creator with certain unalienable rights, and that among these are life, liberty, and the pursuit of happiness."

Second, in the Constitution, America's Founders inverted the understanding of sovereignty. Power comes not from the top down, but up, from "We the People," and governing authority for those in political office is limited to set periods subject to elections. As James Madison explained in Federalist 51: "If men were angels, no government would be necessary. . . . In framing a government which is to be administered by men over men, the great difficulty lies in this: you must first enable the government to control the governed; and in the next place oblige it to control itself."

Even from my short time in elected office, I can assure you that there are no angels in Washington, D.C. And that is why Thomas Jefferson said the "chains of the Constitution" should bind the mischief of government. Only when government is limited are rights protected, the rule of law honored, and freedom allowed to flourish.

You who are graduating from Hillsdale are familiar with these ideas. As the late conservative writer and educator Russell Kirk observed, "Hillsdale does not subscribe to the notion that all books published before 1900 are obsolete. Against all odds, the College speaks up—as it did during the nineteenth century—for 'permanent things.'" And with those as our foundation, what has freedom wrought?

Simply put, the American free market system is the greatest engine for prosperity and opportunity that the world has ever seen. Freedom works. No other nation on Earth has allowed so many millions to come with nothing and achieve so much. In the centuries before the American Revolution, the average human lived on between one and three dollars a day, no matter whether one lived in Europe, Asia, Africa, or North or South America. But from that point on—from the beginning of the American experiment—for the first time in human history, per capita income in a few countries began to grow rapidly, and nowhere more so than in the United States.

Over the last two centuries, U.S. growth rates have far outpaced growth rates throughout the world, producing per capita incomes about six times greater than the world average and 50 percent higher than those in Europe. Put another way, the United States holds 4.5 percent of the world's population, and produces a staggering 22 percent of the world's output—a fraction that has remained stable for two decades, despite growing competition from around the world.

This predominance isn't new. The late British economist Angus Maddison observed that American per capita income was already the highest in the world in the 1830s. This is a result of America's economic freedom, which enables entrepreneurs and small businesses to flourish.

Today the U.S. dollar is the international reserve currency. English is the world's standard language for commerce. The strength of our economy allows us to maintain the mightiest military in the world. And U.S. culture—film, TV, the Internet— is preeminent in the world (although for many of our TV shows and movies, perhaps we owe the world an apology). A disproportionate number of the world's great inventions in medicine, pharmaceuticals, electronics, the Internet, and other technology come from America, improving, expanding, and saving lives. America was where the telephone, the automobile, the airplane, and the iPhone were invented. Americans were the first to walk on the moon.

But most important, freedom produces opportunity. And I would encourage each of you to embrace what I call opportunity conservatism, which means that we should look at and judge every proposed domestic policy with a laser focus on how it impacts the least among us—how it helps the most vulnerable Americans climb the economic ladder.

The political left in our country seeks to reach down the hand of government and move people up the economic ladder. This attempt is almost always driven by noble intentions. And yet it never, ever works. Conservatives, in contrast, understand from experience that the only way to help people climb the economic ladder is to provide them the opportunity to pull themselves up one rung at a time.

As President Reagan said, "How can we love our country and not love our countrymen, and loving them, reach out a hand when they fall, heal them when they're sick, and provide opportunity to make them self-sufficient so they will be equal in fact and not just in theory?"

Historically, our nation has enjoyed remarkable economic mobility. About 60 percent of the households that were in the lowest income quintile in 1999 were in a higher quintile ten years later. During the same decade, almost 40 percent of the richest households fell to a lower quintile. This is a nation where you can rise or fall. It is a nation where you can climb the economic ladder based not on who you are born to, or what class you are born into, but based on your talents, your passion, your perseverance, and the content of your character.

Economic freedom and the prosperity it generates reduce poverty like nothing else. Studies consistently confirm that countries with higher levels of economic freedom have poverty levels that are as much as 75 percent lower than countries that are less free.

Thanks to America's free market system, the average poor American has more living space than the typical non-poor person in Sweden, France, or the United Kingdom. In 1970, the year I was born, only 36 percent of the U.S. population enjoyed air conditioning. Today, 80 percent of poor households in America have air conditioning; and 96 percent of poor parents say that their children were never hungry at any time in the preceding year because they could not afford food.

Now, of course, there is still need in America and throughout the world, and all of us should act to help our fellow man. But more and more government is not the way to do this. To insist otherwise is to ignore the fact that all major European nations have higher levels of public spending than the United States, and that all of them are poorer.

Nor are human beings happiest when they're taken care of by the state. Indeed, areas under the yoke of dependency on government are among the least joyous parts of our society. The story of Julia that we saw depicted in last year's election—the story of cradle-to-grave dependency on government—is not an attractive utopia. Men and women flourish, instead, when afforded the equal opportunity to work and create and accomplish.

I remember some time ago when former Texas senator Phil Gramm was participating in a Senate hearing on socialized medicine, and the witness there explained that government would best take care of people. Senator Gramm gently demurred and said, "I care more about my family than anyone else does." And this wide-eyed witness said, "Oh, no, Senator. I care as much about your children." Senator Gramm smiled and said, "Really? What are their names?"

It is precisely because economic freedom and opportunity outperform centralized planning and regulation that so many millions have risked everything for a chance at the American dream.

Fifty-five years ago, my father fled Cuba, where he had been imprisoned and tortured—including having his teeth kicked out—as a teenager. Today my father is a pastor in Dallas. When he landed in Austin, Texas, in 1957, he was eighteen. He couldn't speak a word of English. He had $100 sewn into his underwear. He went and got a job washing dishes and made 50 cents an hour. He worked seven days a week and paid his way through the University of Texas, and then he got a job, and then he went on to start a small business.

Now imagine if, at that time, the minimum wage had been two dollars an hour. He might never have had the opportunity to get that dishwashing job and work his way through school and work his way up from there. I cannot tell you how many times I've thanked God that some well-meaning liberal didn't greet him when he landed in Austin and put his arm around him and say: "Let me take care of you. Let me make you dependent on government. Let me sap your self-respect—and by the way, don't bother learning English."

When I was a kid, my father used to say to me: "When we faced oppression in Cuba, I had a place to flee to. If we lose our freedom here, where do we go?" For my entire life, my dad has been my hero. But what I find most incredible about his story is how commonplace it is. Every one of us here today has a story like that. We could line up at this podium and each of us tell the story of our parents or grandparents or our great-great-great grandparents. We are all children of those who risked everything for liberty. That's the DNA of what it means to be an American—to value freedom and opportunity above all.

In 1976, Margaret Thatcher delivered her "Britain Awake" speech. In it, she said: "There are moments in our history when we have to make a fundamental choice. This is one such moment, a moment when our choice will determine the life or death of our kind of society and the future of our children. Let's ensure that our children will have cause to rejoice that we did not forsake their freedom."

If we don't fight to preserve our liberty, we will lose it. The men and women graduating here today, blessed with a world-class liberal arts education and a Hillsdale love of learning, are perfectly situated to lead the fight, to tell and retell the story of the miracle of freedom to so many Americans—so many young

Americans in particular—who've never heard that story from the media, or in their schools, and certainly not from Hollywood.

Mrs. Thatcher continued, "Of course, this places a burden on us, but it is one that we must be willing to bear if we want our freedom to survive."

Throughout history, we have carried the torch for freedom. At Hillsdale, you have been prepared to continue to do so, that together we may ensure that America remains a shining city on a hill, a beacon to the world of hope and freedom and opportunity.

Thank you and God bless you.

You Are More Important Than You Know

★

MARY EBERSTADT

Seton Hall University

CLASS OF 2014

MARY EBERSTADT is a writer and senior fellow at the Ethics and Public Policy Center in Washington, D.C. Her appearance was contested by faculty upset with what they deemed her politically incorrect views on parenting.

You have to admit, it's a challenging spring to be a commencement speaker. Some campuses seem to want to tar and feather their invited guests. Meanwhile, pundits keep saying that no one ever remembers commencement speeches anyway. So speakers these days are getting two messages: "We don't like what you say—and, we're not listening to you anyway."

84

But that's a caricature. I know that you are listening, and I want very much to honor your attentiveness and your achievement today by leaving you with some thoughts to remember.

It's especially humbling to share the company up here of Stanislaw Cardinal Dziwisz, who is also receiving an honorary degree. During the last years of the Cold War, right before most of you students were born, I was privileged to serve as a speechwriter to various leaders in the United States government. As those of you who've studied history will know, the people of Poland and the Polish Catholic Church were courage personified during those years. They embodied the principle that truth is truth no matter who says otherwise, and that lies are lies no matter who is telling them, or how often.

And their valiant example taught me, and teaches all of us, something enduring. Protest just for the sake of protest is no difficult thing. Protest just for the sake of protest is like taking a selfie: it's here today, forgotten tomorrow. But protest for the sake of Truth with a capital T is something else—a moral act that if repeated becomes a historical legacy lasting for centuries, like the twentieth-century defeat of totalitarianism. And it's that way of bearing witness that I'm here to talk to you about today.

Pope Francis has been repeating something over and over in recent speeches that goes straight to the heart of what I want to share with you. He says that our moral business as human beings is to see all people, everywhere and at all times, as our brothers and sisters—to see in every individual before us the face of Jesus Christ or God, as he keeps putting it.

Of course not everyone believes in God, though at a

Catholic university one's probably safe in assuming that there are at least some people in His corner. But everybody, religious or otherwise, can understand that Pope Francis is getting at something profound with this image of his. Let's start by noting what he doesn't say. He doesn't say that everyone wears the face of God "except for whoever unfriended you yesterday." He doesn't say everyone wears the face of God "except for the people you disagree with, or think you disagree with, or have been told you ought to disagree with." He doesn't say "except for your student-loan officer." No. He says instead that every human being wears the face of God—no asterisks or footnotes attached.

It's no coincidence that the pope keeps repeating that thought at this moment in time, this very moment when you, the Class of 2014, are moving out and up into a society badly in need of leaders with backbone. My purpose here today is to connect those two things, both the meaning of Pope Francis's insistence, and the meaning of what we might call your own moral footprint on the world. My message amounts to seven simple words: you are more important than you know.

You are more important than you know, first, as members of the families that have lovingly brought you to this place pulsing with happiness. These include your parents or grandparents or great-grandparents who may have immigrated to America, all the hands that rocked your cradles and washed your gym clothes, all the mothers, fathers, sisters, brothers, and others who've lifted you literally and figuratively, from your first car seat to the chairs you occupy here today.

Just as looking at the cardinal a moment ago let us glimpse

the invisible others connected to his presence here today, so does looking out at all of you from this dais reveal the waves of human devotion that brought you to this place. Behind each and every one of you stands an invisible posse stretching from this present moment way back through time. And just as invisible but still present are the other people waiting in the wings of your futures—the marriages you will make, the children you will be privileged to have, the others to whom you will act as mother and father or sister or brother, with or without ties of blood.

Every year, as those of you who have studied behavioral science out there know, we learn more and more about the miraculously social world of animals, especially mammals. Science shows that elephants and orcas and dolphins and others are exquisitely social creatures, more so than was ever understood before, whose well-being depends on their relatedness to others in their group. The same scientific uncovering is true of human animals. Every year, sociology and psychology and anthropology yield up new evidence about the indispensability of your family, especially, to everything about you.

You are more important than you know in another way—as ambassadors of the Judeo-Christian tradition of service to others, no matter where you end up living and what else you end up doing. For this lesson, too, you can thank this great school of yours, again regardless of your own affiliation or beliefs. The Catholic Church, like the Judaism from which it drank, exhibited from its earliest moments a mindfulness toward the poor and worst-off that is without historical peer. Its hundreds of thousands of hospitals, soup kitchens, shelters, schools, hospices, and other homes for humanity's castaways are monuments to a truth that's often ignored these days:

The Church is an immense force for good in the world.

You can be proud of that legacy shared by virtue of your time here—again, whether you are churchgoers yourselves or not. Every time you drop off groceries or calm a sick child, every time you give till it hurts and put your personal gifts at the service of that call to mercy, your worth to those you help will count more than you, or any of us, can possibly know. And specifically to the Catholics among you: be proud of all that, and don't wear a "Kick Me" sign for being Catholic.

You are all more important than you know to the communities you now join on leaving Seton Hall University. Seeing the face of God in every human being isn't only about checking a mental box called "poor people in faraway lands." It's also about thinking globally, and living locally. It's about knowing the names of the people who mow your lawns or clean your offices at night. It's about leaving tips and thank-yous in hotel rooms and restaurants for all the unseen hands that clean up after you. It's about understanding that charity isn't charity when you're using other people's money to do it— it's only charity if you're using your own. Seeing God in every face you meet also means watching our language more closely than many people do—for starters, never, ever using the word "illegal" as a noun to describe a human being.

You are also more important than you know as citizens, residents, and friends of the United States of America to come—right this minute, especially this minute. An insidious new intolerance now snakes its way into classrooms, board-rooms, newsrooms, and other places vital to the exercise of free speech. This new intolerance says we must have diversity in all things—except ideas. It says we must all march in ideo-logical lockstep—or feel the snake bite, and be taken by ambu-lance from the public square. Thirty-six years ago, the towering Russian intellectual Aleksandr Solzhenitsyn delivered a com-mencement address somewhere north of here, and among the things he said was this: "A decline in courage may be the most striking feature that an outside observer notices in the West today." Thirty-six years later, watching the silencings and self-silencings in public life around you, do his words sound overly dramatic—or chillingly prophetic?

The new intolerance insinuates that people who put their faith in a deity are on the wrong side of history. It's up to you, every one of you, to bear witness to this contrary principle: there is no wrong side of history. There is only the wrong side of truth.

You are more important than you know, finally, because of this happy fact: the most underestimated force on the planet may be the power of example, including your own example.

Ten years from now, young people who are children today will be looking up to you for mentorship. Thirty years from now, some of you will be attending a commencement cere-mony like this one, and maybe even in this very place, sitting where your own families sit now, and thinking about the par-ties right around the corner. A hundred years from now, peo-ple who don't exist yet will be remembering you fondly as a coach, a teacher, a neighbor, a friend, a grandfather or grand-mother, and much more.

The ripples of every human action fan out too broadly and in too many directions for our limited mortal eyes to track or map. A priest I know of in Maryland once prayed on his knees in snow outside an abortion clinic—and unbeknownst to him at the time, a woman who was looking out the window that day canceled her planned appointment, and went on to have a baby a few months later. All because she saw this stranger praying in the snow. That priest, like all of you, mattered more than he knew.

You can be proud all your lives of the great ethical truths that you have been taught in this great Catholic university. They aren't arbitrary theological edicts, but universal truths with a claim to every mind and heart. It's good, not bad, to defend the defenseless—the destitute, the castaways, the throwaways—against the powerful and predatory. It's true, and not some-thing to be mumbled with apology, to say that human beings have human dignity and that yes, human dignity means that some things are beneath human beings. If we didn't believe that, we'd have no argument against slavery. It's positive, not negative, to look backward in time to the Roman Empire, say, and to see that the Church started a moral revolution by saying no to female infanticide and yes to the idea that men and women have equal moral worth.

And that last point is especially pressing in a world bent on Roman infanticide 2.0. As of the past couple of decades, mil-lions and millions of baby girls are missing from the face of the earth—because they were disposed of, once a sonogram revealed them to be girls, not boys. All those disappeared girls, all those victims of what some have dubbed global "gender-cide," have faces too. This very month, the world waits anxiously for news about the teenaged schoolgirls of Nigeria, kidnapped from their very dormitories by brute force and held captive in defiance of every legal and moral norm. Everyone here stands with them, and everyone here can connect the moral dots between these twin transgressions: if it's wrong to kidnap girls because they are girls, it's wrong to abort girls because they are girls, too.

In standing up for truths like these, in protesting politely but forcefully on behalf of them, yours are absolutely vital voices in the years ahead. You are all, if you want it, part of the new moral movement that Pope Francis seems to be calling for between the lines of his speeches. It's a movement of empathy for everybody, in an age where empathy was never needed more. It's a movement that sees human faces for what they are—not only where they're obvious, but also where others don't. As graduates of a university that stands by all these things, as foot soldiers and officers in the making of this moral movement now being born, you can be proud of your work on its behalf for all time to come—just as your family and teachers and well-wishers everywhere will never forget how proud we all are of you today. Thank you.

What You Make of Yourself Is Your Gift to God

★

CARLY FIORINA

North Carolina Agricultural and Technical State University

Class of 2005

CARLY FIORINA is the former chief executive officer of Hewlett-Packard. She is the first woman to lead a Fortune 20 company. Fiorina worked for John McCain's 2008 presidential campaign, and ran for the U.S. Senate in California in 2010.

The purpose of a commencement speaker is to dispense wisdom. But the older I get, the more I realize that the most important wisdom I've learned in life has come from my mother and my father. Before we go any further, let's hear it one more time for your mothers and mother figures, fathers and father figures, family, and friends in the audience today.

When I first received the invitation to speak here, I was the CEO of an $80 billion Fortune 11 company with 145,000 employees in 178 countries around the world. I held that job for nearly six years. It was also a company that hired its fair share of graduates from North Carolina A&T. You could always tell who they were. For some reason, they were the ones that had stickers on their desks that read, "Beat the Eagles."

But as you may have heard, I don't have that job anymore. After the news of my departure broke, I called the school, and asked: do you still want me to come and be your commencement speaker? Chancellor Renick put my fears to rest. He said, "Carly, if anything, you probably have more in common with these students now than you did before." And he's right. After all, I've been working on my résumé. I've been lining up my references. I bought a new interview suit. If there are any recruiters here, I'll be free around eleven.

I want to thank you for having me anyway. This is the first public appearance I've made since I left HP. I wanted very much to be here because this school has always been set apart by something that I've believed very deeply; something that takes me back to the earliest memories I have in life. One day at church, my mother gave me a small coaster with a saying on it. During my entire childhood, I kept this saying in front of me on a small desk in my room. In fact, I can still show you that coaster today. It says: "What you are is God's gift to you. What you make of yourself is your gift to God."

Those words have had a huge impact on me to this day. What this school and I believe in very deeply is that when we think about our lives, we shouldn't be limited by other people's stereotypes or bigotry. Instead, we should be motivated by our own sense of possibility. We should be motivated by our own sense of accomplishment. We should be motivated by what we believe we can become. Jesse Jackson has taught us; Ronald McNair taught us; the Greensboro Four taught us; that the people who focus on possibilities achieve much more in life than people who focus on limitations.

The question for all of you today is: how will you define what you make of yourself?

To me, what you make of yourself is actually two questions. There's the "you" that people see on the outside. And that's how most people will judge you, because it's all they can see—what you become in life, whether you were made president of this, or CEO of that, the visible you.

But then, there's the invisible you, the "you" on the inside. That's the person that only you and God can see. For twenty-five years, when people have asked me for career advice, what I always tell them is don't give up what you have inside. Never sell your soul—because no one can ever pay you back.

What I mean by not selling your soul is don't be someone you're not, don't be less than you are, don't give up what you believe, because whatever the consequences that may seem scary or bad—whatever the consequences of staying true to yourself are—they are much better than the consequences of selling your soul.

You have been tested mightily in your life to get to this moment. And all of you know much better than I do: from the moment you leave this campus, you will be tested. You will be tested because you won't fit some people's preconceived notions or stereotypes of what you're supposed to be, of who you're supposed to be. People will have stereotypes of what you can or can't do, of what you will or won't do, of what you should or shouldn't do. But they only have power over you if you let them have power over you.

They can only have control if you let them have control, if you give up what's inside. I speak from experience. I've been there. I've been there, in admittedly vastly different ways—and in many ways, in the fears in my heart, exactly the same places. The truth is I've struggled to have that sense of control since the day I left college. I was afraid the day I graduated from college. I was afraid of what people would think.

Afraid I couldn't measure up. I was afraid of making the wrong choices. I was afraid of disappointing the people who had worked so hard to send me to college. I had graduated with a degree in medieval history and philosophy. If you had a job that required knowledge of Copernicus or twelfth-century European monks, I was your person. But that job market wasn't very strong.

So, I was planning to go to law school, not because it was a lifelong dream—because I thought it was expected of me. Because I realized that I could never be the artist my mother was, so I would try to be the lawyer my father was. So, I went off to law school. For the first three months, I barely slept. I had a blinding headache every day. And I can tell you exactly which shower tile I was looking at in my parents' bathroom on a trip home when it hit me like a lightning bolt. This is my life. I can do what I want. I have control. I walked downstairs and said, "I quit."

I will give my parents credit in some ways. That was 1976. They could have said, "Oh well, you can get married." Instead, they said, "We're worried that you'll never amount to anything." It took me a while to prove them wrong. My first job was working for a brokerage firm. I had a title. It was not "VP." It was "receptionist." I answered phones, I typed, I filed. I did that for a year. And then, I went and lived in Italy, teaching English to Italian businessmen and their families. I discovered that I liked business. I liked the pragmatism of it; the pace of it. Even though it hadn't been my goal, I became a businessperson.

I like big challenges, and the career path I chose for myself at the beginning was in one of the most male-dominated professions in America. I went to work for AT&T. It didn't take me long to realize that there were many people there who didn't have my best interests at heart.

I began my career as a first-level salesperson within AT&T's long lines department. Now, "long lines" is what we used to call the long-distance business, but I used to refer to the management team at AT&T as the "42 longs"—which was their suit size, and all those suits—and faces—looked the same.

I'll never forget the first time my boss at the time introduced me to a client. With a straight face, he said, "This is Carly Fiorina, our token bimbo." I laughed, I did my best to dazzle the client, and then I went to the boss when the meeting was over and said, "You will never do that to me again."

In those early days, I was put in a program at the time called the Management Development Program. It was sort of an accelerated up-or-out program, and I was thrown into the middle of a group of all male sales managers who had been there quite a long time, and they thought it was their job to show me a thing or two. A client was coming to town and we had decided that we were getting together for lunch to introduce me to this customer who was important to one of my accounts.

Now the day before this meeting was to occur, one of my male colleagues came to me and said, "You know, Carly, I'm really sorry. I know we've had this planned for a long time, but this customer has a favorite restaurant here in Washington, D.C., and they really want to go to that restaurant, and we need to do what the customer wants, and so I don't think you'll be able to join us."

"Why is that?" I asked. Well, the restaurant was called the Board Room. Now, the Board Room back then was a restaurant on Vermont Avenue in Washington, D.C., and it was a strip club. In fact, it was famous because the young women who worked there would wear these completely see-through baby doll negligees, and they would dance on top of the tables while the patrons ate lunch.

The customer wanted to go there, and so my male colleagues were going there. So I thought about it for about two hours. I remember sitting in the ladies' room thinking, "Oh God, what am I going to do?" And finally I came back and said, "You know, I hope it won't make you too uncomfortable, but I think I'm going to come to lunch anyway."

Now, I have to tell you I was scared to death. So the morning arrived when I had to go to the Board Room and meet my client, and I chose my outfit carefully. I dressed in my most conservative suit. I carried a briefcase like a shield of honor. I got in a cab. When I told the taxi driver where I wanted to go he whipped around in his seat and said, "You're kidding, right?" I think he thought I was a new act.

In any event, I arrived, I got out, I took a deep breath, I straightened my bow tie, and went in the door—and you have to picture this—I go into the door, there's a long bar down one side, there's a stage right in front of me, and my colleagues are sitting way on the other side of the room. And there's a live act going on the stage. The only way I could get to them was to walk along that stage. I did. I looked like a complete idiot. I sat down, we had lunch.

Now, there are two ends to that story. One is that my male colleagues never did that to me again. But the other end to the story, which I still find inspiring, is that all throughout lunch they kept trying to get those young women to dance in their negligees on top of our table—and every one of those young women came over, looked the situation over and said, "Not until the lady leaves."

It even followed me to HP. As you may know, the legend of HP is that it began in a garage. When I took over, we launched a get-back-to-basics campaign we called "the rules of the garage." A fellow CEO at a competitor saw that and decided to do a skit about me. In front of the entire financial analyst and media community, he had an actress come out with blond hair and long red nails and flashy clothes, and had a garage fall on her head. It made big headlines locally. It made me feel a lot like the "token bimbo" all over again.

I know all of you have your own stories. When you challenge other people's ideas of who or how you should be, they may try to diminish and disgrace you. It can happen in small ways in hidden places, or in big ways on a world stage. You can spend a lifetime resenting the tests, angry about the slights and the injustices. Or, you can rise above it.

People's ideas and fears can make them small—but they cannot make you small. People's prejudices can diminish them—but they cannot diminish you. Small-minded people can think they determine your worth. But only you can determine your worth. At every step along the way, your soul will be tested. Every test you pass will make you stronger.

But let's not be naïve. Sometimes, there are consequences to not selling your soul. Sometimes, there are consequences to staying true to what you believe. And sometimes, those consequences are very difficult. But as long as you understand the consequences and accept the consequences, you are not only stronger as a result, you're more at peace.

Many people have asked me how I feel now that I've lost my job. The truth is, I'm proud of the life I've lived so far, and though I've made my share of mistakes, I have no regrets. The worst thing I could have imagined happened. I lost my job in the most public way possible, and the press had a field day with it all over the world. And guess what? I'm still here. I am at peace and my soul is intact. I could have given it away and the story would be different. But I heard the word of Scripture in my head: "What benefit will it be to you if you gain the whole world, but lose your soul?"

When people have stereotypes of what you can't do, show them what you can do. When they have stereotypes of what you won't do, show them what you will do. Every time you pass these tests, you learn more about yourself. Every time you resist someone else's smaller notion of who you really are, you test your courage and your endurance. Each time you endure, and stay true to yourself, you become stronger and better. I do not know any of you personally. But as a businessperson and a former CEO, I know that people who have learned to overcome much can achieve more than people who've never been tested. And I do know that this school has prepared you well. After all, North Carolina A&T graduates more African Americans with engineering degrees than any other school in the United States. It graduates more African American technology professionals than any other school. It graduates more African American women who go into careers in science, math, and technology than any other school. Your motto is right.

North Carolina A&T is truly a national resource and a local treasure. And Aggie Pride is not just a slogan—it's a hard-earned fact! Never sell your education short. And the fact that this school believed in you means you should never sell yourself short. What I have learned in twenty-five years of managing people is that everyone possesses more potential than they realize. Living life defined by your own sense of possibility, not by others' notions of limitations, is the path to success.

Starting today, you are one of the most promising things America has to offer: you are an Aggie with a degree. My hope is that you live life defined by your own sense of possibility, your own sense of worth, your own sense of your soul. Define yourself for yourself, not by how others are going to define you—and then stick to it. Find your own internal compass. I use the term "compass," because what does a compass do? When the winds are howling, and the storm raging, and the sky is so cloudy you have nothing to navigate by, a compass tells you where true north is. And I think when you are in a lonely situation, you have to rely on that compass. Who am I? What do I believe? Do I believe I am doing the right thing for the right reason in the best way that I can? Sometimes, that's all you have. And always, it will be enough.

Most people will judge you by what they see on the outside. Only you and God will know what's on the inside. But at the end of your life, if people ask you what your greatest accomplishment was, my guess is, it will be something that happened inside you, that no one else ever saw, something that had nothing to do with outside success, and everything to do with how you decide to live in the world.

What you are today is God's gift to you. What you make of yourself is your gift to God.

He is waiting for that gift right now. Make it something extraordinary.

RESTORE AND REMAKE OUR COUNTRY

★

VICTOR DAVIS HANSON

School of Public Policy at Pepperdine University

CLASS OF 2014

VICTOR DAVIS HANSON is a military historian and classicist. He is a senior fellow at the Hoover Institution, a frequent contributor to the *National Review* and other publications, and a prolific author.

Each generation of Americans has always been judged. Did our country under their leadership progress morally, politically, and economically or languish and fall into decline?

On the eve of the Civil War, a failed establishment could not prevent that horrific conflict. But a younger generation was asked to fight it. And indeed untested young officers and soldiers of the North won the conflict for the idea of greater freedom and a more perfect Union. That same generation, veterans of that terrible war, soon came of age to reinvent America in the latter nineteenth century into a world power—one unsurpassed in its productive, financial, and scientific genius. From the cauldron of Antietam and Shiloh came the Golden Age of Bell, Edison, and the Wright brothers.

Yet out of the new affluence, another generation, too complacent and too smug, once again almost lost the United States in the 1920s and 1930s. Their legacies were the frivolities of the Roaring Twenties whose excesses led to the Great Depression—with all its extremist ideologies, and the isolationism that helped bring on World War II.

Then once again, a very different, younger group of Americans, with a terrible inheritance of poverty, and then war, rose to confront the crisis. Like those who came of age in 1861, the Greatest Generation at D-Day and Okinawa once again saved the United States. They went on to contain communism. They rebuilt a postwar world out of ashes. They began needed civil rights reform at home. Your grandparents' cohort passed on to us, the Baby Boomers, a richer, stronger, better America, born into unprecedented peace and prosperity.

Yet for all our self-congratulation, for all our now accustomed first-person self-referencing, we of the present "me" establishment have, I fear, failed our promise and not matched our accustomed boasts. Let us be frank: We are passing on to you graduates an America now mired in $18 trillion of aggregate debt. It is torn apart by red and blue political divisions, ethnic tensions, and class warfare—in elective decline as a world power, without confidence in moral values and prone to accept fad in lieu of religious belief.

That is a bleak diagnosis on this beautiful Malibu beach morning. But it is one nevertheless that is true and therefore demands to be spoken as true. Indeed, you of this graduating class belong to a generation saddled with $1 trillion in student debt. It is you who are asked to subsidize the new health care and social security burdens of my wealthier generation. We will demand in our dotage services from you that we ourselves are now not willing to pay for.

Yet I believe our present youth—you of this graduating class of the School of Public Policy at Pepperdine—like those untried youth of the nineteenth century and those inexperienced who prevailed in the twentieth amid depression and war, can be America's great hope. For all the caricatures of the millennials glued to video games, or camped out in Mom's basement, or sipping hot chocolate in pajamas, already we are seeing evidence that many of you do not accept the ideologies and conformism of a now politicized university that has charged you much, and yet so often imparted to you so little in return. The causes of hope are everywhere.

We must remember also that no military in the world could have fought better than did our youth in Afghanistan and Iraq—if only my generation of leaders had matched their bravery with inspired leadership. The bravery of your cohort is already rejecting my generation's easy orthodoxies that suggested that family, marriage, child raising, and values of the past were passé, as if America had to reinvent itself to be perfect to be good. And yet of all the nations of the Industrial West, America alone will have a chance to avoid the plague of depopulation, an old Western disease that is brought about by affluence, leisure, atheism, and state socialism.

Once again, you do not believe that the color of one's skin, but only the content of one's character is all that matters to be an American. Your generation, unlike mine, is not berating our wonderful Constitution. But for the first time in decades young people are appreciating its genius, a form of government unlike any in the world.

In your time, the United States will become the greatest producer of energy in the history of civilization, brought about by genius and audacity that can find expression alone in a free enterprise system. So there is much to be optimistic about this chapter of America that may well be on the cusp of a great Reawakening, a Renaissance, one that must be led by you, as emblemized by this graduating class. You, who grew up with national debt, with student debt, and with budget debt, will likewise, I believe, once more insist on American solvency and pledge to pay off the debts of my generation so that you do not leave liabilities for your children the way we tragically left them for you. Indeed, you will have no choice but to do precisely that.

Already young people in high technology, in agriculture, in energy, and in new manufacturing are looking at the world anew, without the prejudices and ideological straitjackets of those who tried to fundamentally transform America in their own jaded images of the 1960s and 1970s. So do not despair of your debt. Do not give in to the current nihilism, sarcasm, and cynicism of the elite American coastal establishment. Question the politically correct dogmas of our age; return to older notions of what made America singular. You can become the classically liberal generation; rather than mine that proved to be the stereotypically reactionary one.

Remember instead that you have been given a great gift, even amid your inheritance of debt and decline and social divisiveness and cultural acrimony. The Greeks and the Romans believed that only with material hardship and challenge could courage and genius rise to the occasion. Moral progress often emerges from material regress. So also you have the chance to rise to the occasion like the other favored generations of Americans, and you can earn the gratitude and appreciation of your elders for renewing America in a way we could not.

I am convinced of that. Take up the challenge—2014 graduating class of the School of Public Policy at Pepperdine—and restore and remake our country with just that confidence.

BE FAITHFUL IN THE
SMALL THINGS

★

BRIT HUME

Randolph-Macon College

CLASS OF 2014

BRIT HUME is the senior political analyst for FOX
News, where he previously hosted *Special Report with Brit
Hume*. Hume also served as a correspondent for ABC
News from 1976 to 1996, and as its chief White House
correspondent for the last seven of those years.

I want to tell you about someone. When I was a correspondent in the Washington bureau of ABC News back in the
1980s, a young woman came to us from the University of Virginia where I went. I don't think I would have known that she
went there if we hadn't had that in common and talked about it.
And she took an entry-level job at our bureau. And that meant
that she did the lowliest of jobs. She went out for coffee. She did

Xeroxing. She answered the telephone. There's a lot of that in entry-level jobs. But she did all these jobs with uncommon cheer. She did them very well. She got them right. And she was, on top of that, cheerful. She was wonderful on the telephone. And everybody loved her. Her name was Katie Couric.

And I mention that to illustrate a point I want to make to you graduates today, and that is that you are about to leave the world where you are seniors, you are graduates, you are the top of the school, and you are about to enter the work world, which is a very different place. And you will find that success in America is very democratic, with a small "d." It is open to nearly all. And the education you receive at Randolph-Macon will never leave you. The habits of thought, the things you learn, will be with you always. Nobody will ever take them away from you. But the fact that you went here as opposed to somewhere else and received one degree as opposed to another will cease very quickly to matter.

In fact, once you start in the work world it really won't matter very much at all. Because in the work world you'll be working under people who are busy. And what they're looking for is someone who can help them. And you will be assigned, in all likelihood—whether it's a new job or an internship (many of you will go to internships; this is a tough job market, and I understand that)—to a lot of small jobs.

And I heartily recommend to you that you do these small jobs, however tedious and boring they will be, as well as you possibly can. Because whatever the job is, however menial it may seem, it matters to someone above you that it be done properly. And if you do so and do it cheerfully and well, it will be noticed.

It will especially be noticed in such small things as your phone manners. Now, telephones I know are being used in ways different from the ways they used to be. Landlines are going away, and everybody is carrying a phone in their pocket or their hip. They're communicating as much by text as by voice. I understand that. But in any new job in any office you're going to be answering the telephone. When you do you have a wonderful opportunity that you may not recognize to distinguish yourself from others, and that is by having terrific phone manners.

Now, my father used to say to me, when I was in my teenage years, he hated the way I answered the phone. He'd say, "Look, put a little music in your voice." I would answer the phone, "Hello" (mumbling). Or some of you in your early jobs, depending on where you are, "Hello! Good morning. Al's Body Shop. This is Steve." "Al's Body Shop. This is Ellen."

The reason why that's important is that it's cheerful, and it makes a good impression. But the other thing is you don't know who's on the other end of the phone. And if you respond well and with a cheerful greeting and are exceedingly polite to the person on the other end of the phone, and you take a message if you must and you call that person by name, that person is going to be impressed with you. Because an awful lot of young people don't do that. So think about that.

Small jobs, I should tell you, can lead to big jobs. That's a small job. But you never know where it might lead you.

In fact, I learned a hard lesson in phone manners back in my ABC News days. I was covering the transition from the

Bush administration to the Clinton administration. I was in Little Rock, Arkansas. In those days I had covered President Bush in his unsuccessful reelection bid. And my colleague, the famous—perhaps not to you graduates, because this is a long time ago—the very famous, very boisterous Sam Donaldson had covered the Clinton campaign.

And I went over to pick up Clinton and Sam went back to Washington. I was sitting in the work space that we were using in our affiliate station in Little Rock one day. We had a telephone system set up for us where somebody was answering the phones and I got paged. I picked up the phone. They said, "You have a phone call." "Who is it?" I said. And the voice said, "It's Charlton Heston." Some of you may not have heard of Charlton Heston, but he was an extremely famous and successful actor. He played in huge movies—*Ben-Hur*, and other famous movies of that era.

I no more thought this was Charlton Heston than the man on the moon. I assumed it was Sam Donaldson calling. So I picked up the phone and I said, "What the F do you want?" And I didn't say "F." The voice on the other end said, "Mr. Hume, this is Chuck Heston." And I said, "Oh my God."

Well, it turned out, Charlton Heston was a conservative, and he was going to be on the panel at some conference the political journal *National Review* was hosting. And he wanted me to be on the panel. By this time I was stammering, "Mr. Heston." He said, "Brit, please call me Chuck." And I said, "I could no more call you Chuck, sir, than I could call Moses 'Mo.'"

So I learned a hard lesson about phone manners. Believe it

or not, they're important and so are all the other little jobs that you will be assigned to. So keep that in mind as you go.

The other thing I want to mention to you that I think is important is, when you're young, particularly in your twenties, time goes by so slowly. One of my granddaughters just turned fifteen. And there's a picture of me holding her as an infant, and it seems to me like it was about three or four years ago. As you get older time goes by more quickly. And the people you're working for are experiencing time more quickly in those early years than you will be. And there's a temptation sometimes to think the world is passing you by.

You have a job and you've had it awhile, and you think you've learned all you can learn from it. You'll think, "Wow, I need to move on," and maybe you do. Very often you work someplace for a while and you're doing a good job, and the people you're working for are very happy with it. Maybe they want to keep you in that job, and you may not get the advancement you deserve. Sometimes you just have to pick up and go and move on to something else.

But be careful with that because time will hang heavy on your hands. And there's a temptation to believe, "Oh, no, the world is passing me by."

There's an old saying that opportunity only knocks once. That's bunk. The same opportunity may only knock once, but, in America, if you're working hard and trying hard, all kinds of opportunities will come, and it's very important that you choose the right ones. In fact, most people who have been very successful will look back and tell you that some of the best decisions they made were the jobs they didn't take. So it's something to think about.

If you decide—and it's hard to do this in your twenties—I, as President Lindgren described, was extremely lucky. When I started the first job, it turned out to be the business I've been in ever since.

I've never been anything but a reporter.

But some of you won't be so fortunate. You will spend the time trying to get your foot on the bottom rung of the right ladder. But once you do, what you want to think about in terms of advancement and work is trying to learn from the job you have. And if you still have things to learn from the job you have, don't be in a great hurry to move on to the next job. Because if you move around a lot it can look, on a résumé, like you're someone who can't hold a job.

Now that's not as true today as it might once have been because the fluidity of the job market is greater than it once had been. People move along more quickly. The whole pace of life in America has changed from what it once was. But it's something to keep in mind. Opportunity will knock many times in many different ways. Not only once.

So the question as you sit here today about to receive these degrees is: what's it worth to have a college degree? As I mentioned earlier, the habits instilled and the things you've learned will stay with you always. But where you went to college will cease to matter.

But in terms of difficulties, this is where I say a special word, congratulations to the parents. College is expensive. Parents sacrifice for this. And the question arising is, is it worth it? Well, there's new data out on that. Last year college graduates on average in America made 98 percent more money than nongraduates. Think about that, over the course of a career it has been calculated that a college graduate will earn, on average, $500,000 more than a nongraduate. If you look at it that way, college is a bargain.

And another thing to think about as you depart here today: $500,000 is a lot of money. Hell, you're already rich.

BE SALT AND LIGHT

★

BOBBY JINDAL

Liberty University

CLASS OF 2014

BOBBY JINDAL is the governor of Louisiana. He is the son of Indian immigrants, converted to Christianity as a teenager, and is a practicing Catholic. He is an increasingly prominent figure in the Republican Party.

I thought about giving you a speech today lecturing you about going out into the world and working hard and all that stuff. But I got bored with that. I thought about giving you a speech talking about all the great things that are happening in Louisiana, but I knew you'd be bored with that. I thought about giving you a speech talking about how if you like your health care plan, you can keep your health care plan. But I decided I didn't want to lie to you today. I thought about telling you that debt is good, redistribution of wealth is smart, and personal morality doesn't matter anymore. But you only need to know those things if you're planning to go to work for the federal government in Washington, D.C.

Instead, let me start by telling you a few things about my personal story. My parents immigrated to this great country nearly half a century ago. They came without much, but they had heard about the idea of America. And that's what America really is—it's an idea, and the central tenet of that idea is freedom. When my folks arrived in Baton Rouge, Louisiana, in 1971, my mother was already pregnant with me. I was what you would politely call a preexisting condition. My dad didn't look around for handouts, or for the government to pay the hospital bill. No, instead, he worked out paying for me on an installment plan. And, indeed, shortly after I was born, he asked the hospital if they would take me back if he skipped a payment. He was hopeful, but they said no, he was stuck with me.

My dad grew up dirt poor. He was the only one in a large family of nine to get past the fifth grade. But he knew the idea of America was if you work hard, if you apply yourself, you'll be successful. When he got to Baton Rouge, he decided to get a job. He simply went through the yellow pages calling company after company. He finally wore a guy down on the phone from the railroad company, which is pretty amazing when you consider the fact that my dad's got an accent. . . . He not only convinced the guy to hire him, but he told the guy, who said he could start on Monday, "Well, that's great. I don't have a car, I don't have a driver's license." So he tells his new boss, "You're going to have to pick me up on the way to work Monday morning."

I could tell you a lot of amusing stories about my folks adjusting to life in America. But I want to fast forward to the most significant thing that has ever happened to me. It happened when I was a child. A friend I knew gave me a rather odd Christmas present that year. He gave me my very first copy of the Bible. Sometime later, a girl I knew invited me to church. Here I was, looking for a date. She was looking to save my soul. I found the gospel message intriguing, but, I'll be honest, I was skeptical. I'm an analytical sort of person; I decided I'd have to investigate all these fanciful claims. I started reading this Bible, oftentimes hiding in my closet, not sure how my parents would respond. The short story is this—I read the words of Jesus Christ, and I realized they were true. I used to say I found God, but I think it's more accurate to say he found me. And it happened because there were people brave enough to plant the seeds of the gospel in my life.

Many years later, I became a candidate for political office. In one of my first debates, I got this question: "What was the single most important moment in your life?" Now, I'd just endured countless hours of debate prep sessions with my political consultants and staff. That's basically, you get to sit around and be savagely grilled by the people you pay, your political consultants and staffers. I knew exactly what they hoped I would say. They argued I should try to appeal to female voters by offering a touching story about when I asked Supriya, my wife, for her hand in marriage. Or about the birth of our first child, a beautiful baby girl. And yes, those were great moments. But I decided to do something new in politics. I told the audience the truth that day. That the most significant moment in my life was the moment I accepted Jesus Christ as my personal Lord and savior.

My political consultants began shifting uncomfortably in their seats. I've got to admit, I enjoyed that moment. I thought of Matthew 10:33, which says, "Whoever denies me before men, I will also deny him before my father who is in heaven." Or of Romans 1:16, which says, "I'm not ashamed of the gospel, because it is the power of God that brings salvation to everyone who believes." Now it is said that college is an intellectual pursuit involving reason and logic. I went to Brown University in the Ivy League, as you've heard. It is a place that prides itself in intellectual reasoning. One of the good things about going to Brown is that I was quickly able to become president of the college Republicans on campus. The only other Republican student at Brown became the vice president.

Some kids go off to college and lose their way. They become convinced that their faith is not an intellectual pursuit. Nothing could be further from the truth. Reason and logic lead to truth, which means that reason and logic lead to God. There's a general view among many of the elites in America that truly enlightened folks realize that all this faith and religious stuff is just quaint and antiquated thinking from an earlier era. Or that it is a nice, restful place for those who are not as bright or as intellectually curious as they are. Again, nothing could be further from the truth. True intellectual curiosity will inevitably lead to an understanding of our creator.

I've noticed examples of this elitist view of faith when

national political reporters, usually from places like Boston or New York or Washington, D.C., would come to Baton Rouge to interview me in my first years as governor. They, inevitably, in those first interviews, would say something like this: "Governor, you're a smart guy. We know you went to Brown, you're a Rhodes scholar, so tell me—how is it that you call yourself pro-life? How is it that you say you oppose gay marriage? How is it you say you oppose gun control? Be honest—you're just saying that stuff to get elected in the Deep South, right?" So, of course, I like to have a little fun with these reporters. I'd lean over the desk, and in whispered tones, pretending to confide in them, I'd say, "Well, just between us, do me a favor. Go and tell your editor the bad news, tell him I absolutely believe everything I say."

As you can imagine, those interviews ended rather abruptly. They never came back after that, for some reason.

Let me shift gears for a moment, now, and talk straight with you about the world we live in, and about the culture in which our students are about to wade. Today's world is increasingly hostile to matters of faith. American culture has, in many ways, become a secular culture. And at a minimum, to our graduates, it's safe to say you're going into a world that is far more secular than the one your parents entered.

A few months ago, I had the opportunity to speak at the Reagan Library out in California, where I talked about the silent war on religious liberty in America today. The Declaration of Independence says that we are a nation constituted in accordance with the laws of nature and of nature's God, and that we're a people endowed by our creator with certain unalienable rights. Let me make this explicit—the source and justification for the very existence of the United States of America is, and always has been, contingent upon the understanding of Man as a created being, with a creator conferring his intrinsic rights, among them life, liberty, and the pursuit of happiness.

Now, how we understand and approach that creator is properly left to the hearts and consciences of every citizen. For me, I'm a Catholic Christian. My parents? They're Hindus. I'm blessed to know Baptists, Jews, Episcopalians, Presbyterians, and so many more in the rich tapestry of American faiths. I also know men and women who acknowledge no denomination or creed, who confess to uncertainty about the divine yet look to the richness of nature and majesty of this world and wonder and inwardly seek the author of it all.

You know, these days, we think the diversity of belief is tolerated under our law and Constitution. But that's wrong. This diversity of belief is the foundation of our law and Constitution. America does not sustain and create faith. Faith created and sustains America. America did not invent religious freedom. Religious freedom invented America. President John Adams, in 1798, wrote to Massachusetts militiamen to remind them that our Constitution was made only for a moral and religious people. It is wholly inadequate to the government of any other. In 1798, this was simple common sense.

In 2014, we're forced to confront a question that would have been unthinkable to President Adams, or President Washington, or President Reagan or every other American throughout history who believes in America's founding premise. What happens when our government decides it no longer needs a moral and religious people?

Today, the American people, whether they know it or not, are mired in a silent war. It threatens the fabric of our communities, the health of our public square, and the endurance of our constitutional governance. It is a war against the propositions in the Declaration of Independence. It is a war against the spirit that motivated abolitionism. It is a war against the faith that motivated the civil rights struggle. It is a war against the soul of countless acts of charity, it is a war against the conscience that drives social change. It is a war against the heart that binds our neighborhoods together. It is a war against America's best self at America's best moments. It is a war. A silent war against religious liberty.

This war is waged in our courts and the halls of political power. It is pursued with grim and relentless determination by a group of like-minded elites determined to transform our country from a land sustained by faith into a land where faith is silenced, privatized, and circumscribed. Their vision of America is not the vision of the founding. It is not even the vision of ten years ago. It is a vision in which an individual's devotion to Almighty God is accorded about as much respect as a casual hobby and about as many rights and protections. These elites, to this point, have faced little opposition. But there is a remnant who have the temerity to believe in America and her promises and do something about it. My question to our graduates is—will you be a part of that remnant?

Margaret Thatcher famously said this: "Europe was created

by history. America was created by philosophy." The secular elites understand this just as well as she did. They know that to take over America they must make war on this philosophy. This silent war is the real undercurrent driving politically fractious debates and a number of areas of policy. But why is this war happening? What does it mean for the country and people of faith? Why does it represent such a fundamental challenge to our American identity and the exceptional history that makes our nation great? Consider three story lines playing out in our states and the highest courts over the past several years in three different areas, yet all with overlapping effects.

First, the freedom to exercise religion and the way you run your business, large or small, is under assault. You've likely heard of the Obama administration's case against Hobby Lobby, a mega craft store and a family business, whose battle against President Obama's contraception mandate will end up as a Supreme Court decision. The national chain filed suit after being told they would be fined $1.3 million per day if they didn't pay for abortifacients through their insurance.

Hobby Lobby is nothing less than an all-American success story. This company was launched in Oklahoma in 1970 with nothing more than a $600 loan and a workshop in a garage. Today, they have 588 stores in forty-seven states. They have more than thirteen thousand full-time employees. They expanded, branching out to create a Christian supply shop, selling Bibles and craft supplies, opening another thirty-five stores in seven states, with almost four hundred more employees. This is entrepreneurship at its best—a family-owned business that went from $600 in a garage to two companies that employ almost fourteen thousand people, full-time, across the country. Throughout it all, Hobby Lobby has retained the guiding principles of their devout founders. Their statement of purpose begins with a Bible verse, and they're closed every Sunday. They're committed to honor the Lord by being generous employers, paying well above minimum wage, increasing salaries four years in a row, even in the midst of the enduring recession.

None of this matters to the Obama administration. The argument they've advanced successfully thus far is that faithful business owners cannot operate under the assumption that they can use their moral principles to guide the way their places of business spend money. According to the administration's legal arguments, the family that owns Hobby Lobby is not protected by the First Amendment's free exercise of religion clause. That's the part of the First Amendment that states that Congress shall make no law prohibiting the free exercise of religion. The Obama administration and Attorney General Eric Holder argue that Hobby Lobby is a for-profit, secular employer, and a secular entity, by definition, does not exercise religion. A federal judge agreed. Since Hobby Lobby is, quote, a "secular corporation," they have no right to be guided by the religious beliefs of their ownership.

Keep in mind that so-called morning-after pills should be illegal or banned. . . . [Employers] just had a serious moral problem paying for something they viewed as being against their deeply held beliefs. The Obama administration ignores these beliefs, and treats them as little more than an inconvenience to their ever expanding regulatory state.

Let's be clear—this is bigger than Hobby Lobby. The administration's argument strikes at the core of our understanding of free exercise of religion. This case could have enormous ramifications for business owners across our country. Under the Obama regime, you've got the protection of the First Amendment as an individual, you see, but the instant you start a business you lose those protections. And that brings us to the second front of the silent war: the assault on our freedom of association as people of faith, to form organizations where we work alongside others who share our views.

This brings us to the Hosanna-Tabor case, which revolved around the ability of a Lutheran academy in Michigan to fire a teacher. Here, the Obama administration advanced another extreme argument, claiming that job regulations prevented the academy from being able to fire anybody over a difference in beliefs. The lawyers from the Obama administration went far beyond the issues of the case to, instead, advance the legally absurd position that there is no general ministerial exemption, arguing that religious groups don't even have the constitutionally protected right to select their own ministers or rabbis. Thankfully, here, the administration's extreme position was rebutted by the Supreme Court in decisive fashion with a 9–0 decision opposing its perspective.

For the time being, at least, the government doesn't get to decide who can preach the gospel. But the important thing to note is that the government wanted to make that decision. I don't know about you, but to me, that is truly offensive and frightening. The administration advanced that extreme argument because it is consistent with the view of many on the left, particularly elite liberal legal scholars, that the god we must worship first is government. That our rights are doled out by Washington as they see fit. But these cases are only the beginning. There is a bigger threat: the assault on your freedom of expression in all areas of life.

Illinois shows us a preview of what this looks like. In legislation, they proposed altering the definition of marriage. They would require churches and other congregations to essentially close their doors to outsiders, stop providing services to the community, and close off their facilities to other nonprofits and church groups in order to avoid being required to host same-sex ceremonies. They wouldn't allow religious bodies to rent their facilities to nonmembers for use in weddings, for example. They would drive churches to have to eliminate classes, day schools, counseling, fellowship hall meetings, soup kitchens, and much, much more. In other words, this law and others like it would require believers to essentially choose to break with their deeply held theological beliefs, or give up their daily activity of evangelism, retreat from public life, and sacrifice their property rights. This is the next stage of the assault and it is only beginning.

Today, an overwhelming majority of those who belong to a religious denomination in America—that's more than half the country—are members of organizations that affirm the traditional definition of marriage. All of those denominations will be targeted in large and small degrees in the coming years. For example, will churches in America even be able to remain part of the public square in a time when their views on sin are in direct conflict with the culture, and when expressing those views will be seen as hiding, quote, "hateful speech" behind religious protections?

This war on religious liberty, on your freedom to exercise your religion, on your freedom to associate, on your freedom of expression, is only going to continue. It's going to continue because of an idea. A wrongheaded concept. The concept that religious freedom means you have the freedom to worship and that is all. It is the misbegotten and un-American conception of religious liberty that your rights only begin and end in the pew; this is absolutely ridiculous.

We, as Christians, and we, as Americans, have the right to practice our faith and to protect our conscience no matter where we happen to be. But it's also important that we must keep perspective on this silent war. It is certainly a challenging time to be a believer in America, but we must also consider the plight of believers around the world today. In nation after nation, Christians are being slaughtered by radical Islamists for their beliefs. It is a time of enormous upheaval in the Middle East, where your beliefs can lead to your church being burned, your children being kidnapped, or they can put you on the wrong side of a gun.

Dietrich Bonhoeffer wrote this: "The cross is laid on every Christian. It begins with a call to abandon the attachments of the world. When Christ calls a man he bids him to come and die. Today, around the world, many Christians are living out that calling." That is a shooting war over religion, not a silent one.

Here in America, we should be grateful that the laws and principles put in place by the Founders, men like George Mason and James Madison and Patrick Henry, who understood the importance of religious liberty, have endured for so long. They are the reason America has come so far. It is those same principles that should guide us farther still. Principles that understand that power is derived from the people, not from government. Calvin Coolidge understood this in his own time. He said, "We live in an age of science and of abounding accumulation of material things. These do not create our Declaration. Our Declaration created them. The things of the spirit come first. Unless we cling to that, all of our material prosperity, overwhelming though it may appear, will turn to a barren scepter in our grasp."

The president was right. The things of the spirit do come first. We must act and act now to protect them. The temptation, in some corners, is to ask for a truce in these fractious battles. But, in practical terms, a truce would only amount to those who value religious liberty laying down our arms. Our religious freedom was won over centuries of persecution and blood, and we should not surrender it without a fight. Make no mistake—the war over religious liberty is the war over free speech. Without the first, there's no such thing as the second. Though this is not a battle any one of us would have chosen, it is one we are called to join and we should do so gladly, with our hearts and minds set on things above.

left has grown tired of debate. Their new strategy is simply to try to silence their critics. These leftists immediately mobilize. They did all they could not to debate the issues, but rather to attempt to silence the Robertsons. And, as you well know, the same thing happened again just this week with another demonstration of intolerance from the entertainment industry.

HGTV was working on a new show featuring the Benham brothers, twin brothers who graduated from right here at Liberty University in 1998. I know they've been recognized, but I'd like to ask them to stand, and let's give them another round of applause for their courage and grace. HGTV canceled the show this week, allegedly because they learned that one of the brothers had protested at the Democratic Party Convention, and the other had protested at an abortion clinic. I want you to think about that for a minute. If these guys had protested at the Republican Party Convention or here at Liberty University, instead of canceling their show, HGTV would have probably given them a raise and a new deal. There was a time when the left preached tolerance. And the truth is, they still are, indeed, tolerant, unless they happen to disagree with you. To paraphrase William F. Buckley, a liberal is someone who welcomes dissent, and then is astonished to find that there is any.

You know, the modern left in America is completely intolerant to the views of people of faith. They want a completely secular society where people of faith keep their views to themselves. Remember this quote from our fortieth president, President Ronald Reagan, "Freedom is a fragile thing and is never more than one generation away from extinction. It is not ours by inheritance. It must be fought for and defended constantly by each generation." Now, to be clear, churches in America are not being burned to the ground. Christians are not being slaughtered for their faith. There's really no comparison to the persecution of people of faith inside our borders and outside.

We've established that our culture has taken a secular turn. We've established that persecution of Christians is on the rise throughout the world. We've established that religious liberty here, in America, is under siege. We've established that the left no longer wants to debate, they simply want to silence us. So now what? What do we do about it and what should you do about it? First of all, you should be optimistic and be of good cheer. This is an exciting time to be a believer. It is true that Christians are the last group that it is okay to discriminate against in America. But so what? If God is with us, who could be against us?

To the graduates, just a couple of last words of advice—don't see yourself as a victim. America already has enough people who see themselves as victims. Go out into this world. Boldly be salt and light in a world that needs you now more than ever before. Most of all, you should be bold in your faith. Embrace opportunities to stand up for the truth. Just like those people in my life, you never know when you might be planting a seed of the gospel that could change somebody's life for all eternity.

BE PROUD OF AMERICA

★

RUSH LIMBAUGH

The Rush Limbaugh Show

MAY 16, 2008

RUSH LIMBAUGH is the host of the most widely
listened-to talk show in radio history, *The Rush Limbaugh
Show*, where he conducts what he refers to as "The
Limbaugh Institute for Advanced Conservative Studies."
The following is a transcript from a phone call he received
on air from a graduating student at the University of Texas.

CALLER: My question is, what would you say, what
would be your ten-, fifteen-minute speech to all the thousands
of graduates graduating from college campuses across the nation as they go forth to be the future leaders?

RUSH: Excellent question. Before I answer that, I saw somewhere on the Internet a list of the remaining major—not even
major, but I guess division 1, division 1A to put it in a sports con-
text, graduation ceremonies' commencement speakers, and there's

not a damn conservative anywhere. I mean, it's all liberals, some from media, some from the State Department. This is nothing new, by the way. I think P. J. O'Rourke wrote what he would say at Stanford. You know, Jacob, once long ago, I prepared a commencement address way back when I was still in Kansas City, what I would say to students if they were graduating high school. I've thought about it and I've updated it since. Ten to fifteen minutes is tough, but the first thing that I would say is the world does not revolve around you, yet, and you are not the future leaders of this country, yet, just because you've graduated. Now it's up to you to decide what to do with the education that you have. And I would launch into a spirited celebration of the American capitalist system.

I would tell 'em how much of a head start they have over quite a few other people because of their education. Their education was for a purpose. It was to get them into the free market and engage in capitalism and secure the growth of this country because, like their parents, they someday are going to be worried about the future for their kids and they're not going to improve the future of their kids by joining protest marches or wearing ribbons or putting bumper stickers on the backs of their cars. They're going to have to go out, roll up their sleeves, and start working and become productive and further the capitalistic engine of the United States of America. That's how growth is created. I'd probably just continue with that theme. I'd spend some time inspiring them and teaching them a little bit about America to counteract what I thought they had been taught in their classrooms over the course of these past four years or five, depending on how long they've been there. But it would be optimistic, it would be upbeat, it would be positive: You live in the greatest country in the world, and you're gonna hear every day how we're the worst, you're going to hear how we're responsible for global warming and we're destroying the world.

We are not anything but the world's solutions. We are not the problem in the United States of America. I would try to instill in them a pride for being Americans, something that would swell their chests. I would take them through this country and various things that they should be proud of and can be proud of, because it's necessary, because they're going to be bombarded daily, in news, coworkers, and so forth, with people whining and moaning and complaining it can't get done, America is evil, and basically my objective would be optimistic inspiration. I would hope—this is a little bit of a stretch—but I would hope that immediately after the graduation they would eschew the party and head right to a job interview. They wouldn't do it of course, and I want them to go to the party, but love for the country, appreciation for it, understanding their role in it, and someday they are going to be responsible for its greatness, but that has to be earned. It doesn't just come to you because you're an American.

THE SECRET KNOWLEDGE

★

DAVID MAMET

University of Vermont

CLASS OF 2004

DAVID MAMET is a Pulitzer Prize–winning playwright, author, and screenwriter. His works include *Glengarry Glen Ross*, for which he was nominated for a Tony Award.

I was having dinner with my family, the doorbell rang. It was a young man in a hand-me-down suit, selling magazines.

Thank you, I don't want any magazines, I say. I understand, he says, the point of my visit isn't really magazines, it's education. I and a group of underprivileged young people are enrolled in the something-or-other organization, which is chartered as an educational institution. They mean to teach us about success. TO THAT END, we are going into the better neighborhoods, and asking the homeowners questions from which we hope to learn how to succeed. To what do you feel you owe your success?

Well, puff puff puff, and I buy twelve magazine subscriptions off this kid. *Home and Garden, Skiing, Golf,* things I've never done and have no use for. I buy the twelve, and he says if I buy three more, he gets to go to a special motivational seminar in somewhere Colorado, so I buy those three, too. I'm still getting them.

The kid took me down. How dare I go on about "the secret of my success." What an egoistic fool. Whatever success I have I owe, as does anyone, to a combination of luck, genetics, ambition, and perhaps a slight admixture of application. He, the great conman-salesman, offered me a secret thrill cheap. What was the thrill? That I got to pontificate?

Certainly, but I get to do that anyway, I spent twenty years teaching college. The real thrill, I realized much, much later, was this fantasy: that the young actually want to emulate their parents. That they see something admirable in us and in Our Ways. That they want, in effect, "to continue the work we've started." What a bunch of hooey; for they see, and it is perhaps true, that we weren't involved in any "work," but were blundering about, looking for sex, money, fame, adventure, and absolution, just the same as they—your parents, I among them, as I have a daughter graduating from college next week, delude ourselves that you want our help or direction, when a slight application of memory would instruct that you simply want us to get out of your way. Much as we did, when we found ourselves, as the handy phrase has it, "going out into the world."

We looked around, as you do, and we saw the incredible idiot shambles which was and is the world.

And we chafed, as you will, under the yoke of those who had brought the world to this sorry brink, and scorned them and kowtowed to them for various good things to which it seemed they held the key, and we waited for them to die, and learned how to get along with them, and looked back, as we aged, at our young and deluded selves that they could profit from our experience. This delusion is prettified by the term "philosophy," and one of its attendant delusions was exploited by that young man who sold me *Field and Stream*.

Is there no lesson in that interchange?

Yes. That human beings are weak, and suggestible, and, usually, never wronger than when we recur to a philosophy which casts us in the lead.

I recall I told this young fellow that my great success was due, in large part, to my lack of education; that I essentially attended no schools, or if I did, I wasn't paying attention. I think this is true; but as I also thought I was teaching a worthy lesson, and I was actually being conned, must I not consider each part of the transaction suspect, and all my words lies? I think I must.

And, had I actually gotten self-educated, should I not have been able to see through his pretty transparent chicanery? Perhaps it was he who'd gotten the education, and whatever school he'd studied in deserved praise, for it fit him to succeed at that which, for the moment, was his life's work. It took him (and me) right-ways back to the punch-in-the-nose of life.

My hero is Eric Hoffer. He was born in 1902 in Brooklyn to German parents, his mother died when he was young, he was raised in poverty, he went blind from age eight to fifteen, he never spent a day in school, became a hobo, and eventually washed up in San Francisco, where he worked as a longshore-man for twenty-five years.

He worked on the piers by day, at night he wrote the great-est of twentieth-century American philosophy, and I recom-mend his books to you all. Here is a quote from 1967:

"Thus, as the post-industrial age unfolds we begin to suspect that what is waiting for us around the corner is not a novel future, but an immemorial past. It begins to look as if the fabulous cen-tury of the middle class and the middle-aged had been a detour, a wild loop that turns on itself, and ends where it began. We are returning to the rutted highway of history which we left a hun-dred years ago in a mad rush to tame a savage continent and turn it into a cornucopia of plenty. We see all around us the lineaments of a pre-industrial pattern emerging in the post-industrial age. We are rejoining the ancient caravan, a caravan dominated by the myths and magic of elites and powered by the young."

Every civilization in history tries to prepare its young to leave the nest, or, to put it differently, to live in the world. The terror of separation was traditionally dealt with by ceremonies of matricu-lation, the boy child was taken forcibly from the mother, and went to live with the men: the girl child was taken from the family and went to live in the women's hut: the boy went into the military, the girl was initiated into the secrets of sexual or maternal conduct.

In a world filled with awe, the child was forced, say, helped, to substitute respect for fear, to exchange wonder regarding the tribe, the Gods, the universe, for concern about its parents.

"How do I live in the larger world," substituted today by: how may I be spared the necessity.

Options include graduate school, living at home, "Finding Oneself," and other avenues of prolonged and perhaps perpetual adolescence.

In healthier societies the young were imbued with an awe of "the secret knowledge": that knowledge was held out, and revealed, at set periods, to the prepared.

We see these ceremonies persist in: the confirmation, the Bar Mitzvah, military graduation, commencement.

Essential to these ceremonies is the proviso: but you can't come back.

Any ceremony insufficiently strict, whose requirements are other than rigorous, and which permits recidivism, is worthless. I cite, for example, the commitment ceremony rather than marriage—these weak ceremonies do not propel the young toward the pursuit of the secret knowledge. We may call this secret knowledge "God," or, "The mystery of life and death," or "How to comport oneself honorably in a troubling and confusing world," or we may call it marriage, or vocation—but the society which kills, in the young, their desire, their necessity of truly matriculating, is wounding them.

Imagine the baby never encouraged to speak. Why would this child do other than cry?

For what does it cry? For the toy it could have by asking; and for external stringency sufficient to permit it to grow.

Deprived by their guardians of the quest for secret knowledge, the young cannot respect their elders.

If a society is based on consumption, license, and endless

possibility, the young must see their elders as lacking, as they are less strong, supple, and nubile.

There must be inducements to the child, to abandon puerile self-absorption, to matriculate. These inducements are misunderstood as rewards; the true inducement, to the young, however, is not the reward but the task.

These tasks must be capable of accomplishment, but sufficiently stringent to allow the child to complete them with pride.

If he is not tested, he has little reason to abandon the pleasant practices of infancy. Our schools fail, in the main, in being insufficiently rigorous. The latest heresy of education brought on by the mania for testing is that it is essential for the child to graduate. It has been forgotten that the original purpose of the school was to permit the child to learn.

Here is a test by which an education may be judged: may I now employ that which I have supposedly learned to bring about the result the school advertised.

Will the fire bow and socket always produce fire: may I now read Aramaic, play the Mendelssohn.

Much supposed education, instead of imparting skills, exists to blur the distinction between skill and supposition, anesthetizing the young by an assurance that a) all is within them, or b) things are only what they choose to think of them. I am speaking of a liberal arts education, the worth of which, having been subjected to one myself, is still unclear to me. What is the harm in the jollity of deconstructionist literary "theory"? In self-serving application of the term "perhaps."

Perhaps all things are equal, and their only meaning is that which I choose to award them.

Perhaps, then, people are truly good at heart, perhaps the world leaders are acting, appearances to the contrary, in accord with some dedicated plan of public service: perhaps the actions of the Palestinians and the Israelis are somehow equivalent, and perhaps O. J. Simpson did not kill his wife.

Gibbon tells us that the decadence of Roman lawyers was not that they would equally espouse cause A, or B, and claim that either deserved a hearing, and was neither right nor wrong; their decadence was that they came to believe it.

For the nonmatriculated, that person not helped that is, forced to live in the world, to participate in the world which is indeed cruel, but is the only one we have, this person can persist only as one of two things, a child or a victim—for their noninvolvement will not survive the first punch in the nose.

And many would avow that even the murderer deserves an endlessly fair trial, unless, God forbid, the murderer had killed one of one's own.

The charm of a cloistered upbringing is that it inculcates a pleasant sense of self-sufficiency. It is easy to feel self-sufficient if everything has been done for one.

I thought about tattoos. I see that, as most important customs, the tattooing of the young occurs spontaneously and irresistibly. What does it mean? That a person, having obtained a certain amount of years, needs to assert autonomy—other examples include enlisting in the military and cracking up the family car.

We cannot escape from ritual, but the sophisticated call it

by other names—it often seems the automatic outgrowth of personal choice—the billionaire's serial polygamy, the new hairdo following the emptying of the nest.

Each step from one state to the next requires ritual, and if the ritual is not prescribed, it will be invented. We can't come to the phone, but if you will leave a brief message at the tone, we'll get back to you as soon as we can.

This handy phrase came into the language as an incantation in response to an immediate overwhelming phenomenon; just as the stopped motorist cannot resist saying, "Exactly what seems to be the problem, Officer?"

Steps from bondage toward freedom must be accompanied by ritual. Why? Because they pass through terror. Ritual distracts or ameliorates terror as love and sex distract from the shock of union. And the tattoo is an unconscious creation of ritual—"I have altered myself and can never be what I was."

Attempts to escape from the terror of transition lead to stagnation. As shacking up, rather than preparing one for marriage, makes its state less likely, or, if practiced, less possible—as graduate school staves off matriculation into the wider world, and, rather than preparing for it, rehearses the impossibility of success in it. Much of life is a mystery.

Vietnam, we were told, did not repeat the mistake of Korea, and today we are told that Iraq is not another Vietnam. And perhaps history looking back (as it does) will call it inevitable: given D-Day, that the good trick we learned would be repeated until it brought about destruction.

The blessings of a war economy—absent the obscenity of

war—were too great to be discarded, indeed impossible to discard. Without a ceremony. What do we value? Sherlock Holmes taught Watson that, to force the lady to take the most precious stolen documents from the hidden spot in the house, one need only set fire to the house. She'll bring the documents out with her.

What things do we value most—the first love note, the child's first drawing, the Marine tie clasp.

These things are the laurel crown, more precious than gold, more precious than anything, as they mark the blessing or a transformation—which is to say, an experience of the divine—the script binder that held the first play, the ribbon which held a diploma, they are the physical mementos of a mystery.

The sophomore basks in his discovery that the world is plain and blunt—that all is self-interest and hypocrisy, that we are born and then we die. The fortunate young person finds a calling, and calls life a mystery.

Later the mystery palls—work or love become formulaic. One trudges on like a misused automaton; one day the world changes again, we rediscover work or love or religion or children—the love of another, of humanity, and we once again feel the proximity of the divine.

Each new reintroduction of the mystery is preceded by, or accompanied by, pain—we lose a job, a physical ability, a loved one, our illusions, money, possessions, position, and we rally heaven for an explanation.

How, Lord, have I grown old, grown redundant, lost my belief, my physical capabilities?

Age reveals a pattern: self-absorption followed by the possibilities of change.

This possibility contains two questions, the first why was I born, the second thank God I was born. Both of them bring us closer to the divine.

They are unfortunate who never change—the congenitally privileged, the frightened, the arrogant, act, in business, government, and in the home, in an infantile state, as well they might, for they have never left the nursery. They see the world as does the infant, as a machine which is functioning acceptably only when it grants their every wish.

Corporate malfeasance, governmental corruption, and other crimes are the product of an immature mind, which never underwent transformation, knowing only bloated repletion or rage.

In the infant of every age, power breeds corruption; license leads to arrogance, and on to crime. For the licensed individual, like Nebuchadnezzar, wants more, and the more he receives the less it pleases, until, at length, he goes mad and eats grass.

Why does this unmatriculated individual lust for more and more? He knows what he has is worthless.

The new Marine does not want another tie clasp to signify his or her transformation, the birdwatcher having viewed a pileated woodpecker does not burn to have seen two. Those blessed by change—having passed through trial from stasis to a new freedom, these are transmogrified, they have become something new—shocked and blessed to discover they had the ability to grow, they crave the opportunity to repeat that experience, which, they discover, had been one of devotion.

Devotion brings blessing. We like to think, in our weakness, that blessing resides in power, comfort, accumulation, conquest. This is just our good human trick of naming the lesser road the higher, the easier task the more difficult, coupling self-delusion to self-indulgence.

We repeat habitually those experiences which are unenjoyable. Cigarette addiction, serial monogamy, international arrogance.

The world has changed, and we search for the perfect country to invade, hoping its discovery might bring us back to the glory of D-Day, as we hope that endless compulsive dating might help us find the perfect mate—the fault in each, however, lies not in the lack of cooperation of the external world, but in our delusion.

For in geopolitics, as in sex and the city, we always find, magically, there is a fatal flaw—our intended has not read Trollope, or the invaded country, magically, has its own ideas of destiny. Just when everything was going so well.

How do we wean ourselves from the pattern of repetition, of addiction? It requires a shock. This shock, administered by society-at-large, used to be known as ritual. Which we see before us, here today. The ritual of Graduation means, in effect, "Get out." If it does not mean "get out," what might it mean?

Some, understandably, both in the School, and among the students, get addicted to the pleasant process, and wish to prolong it indefinitely, like combatants recovering from honorable wounds who have, unfortunately, become addicted to opiates.

The opiate is difficult to kick, and how may the individual remind him or herself that the pleasant and drowsy interlude of collegial license evolved to dull the difficult transition from adolescence to independence, which is to say, responsibility?

"Get out."

The marriage ceremony, much as it celebrates a union of The Two, might be said, also, to enforce a division: of the groom from the best man, the bride from her retinue, the couple from their parents—the ritual proclaiming to the community, LEAVE THEM ALONE.

If we search for the overlooked in the ceremony, the unacknowledged, there we will find, perhaps, its true meaning. The true meaning must be hidden—or it cannot be operative. If it is conscious, it must be rejected.

(The ritual of tattooing, I suspect, owes much of its popularity to the pain it entails, the actual tattoo image, perhaps, merely a visible sign that the wearer has undergone pain.)

E.g.: A first, adolescent date, which in my day ran: Would you like to have a soda, which must be translated as: I understand if I am to enjoy your company I must feed you—the ritual at the drugstore taking us back to Neanderthal times. And what of the graduation ceremony? What is the hidden, the overlooked element?

It resides, in one place, in this speech, which, operationally, might mean: I will listen to this boring drivel Just One More Time, my demeanor proof that I have learned, in four years of college, to put up with the bombast of the aged. ONE MORE TIME, and then I'm done.

Ritually, in effect, the ceremony is debased, for even my prosing is insufficiently painful to drive you forever from the protection of academia. In a better ritual, you would have to drag your diploma, that is, your quittance, from a burning pyre, to scar your-selves, to prove that you could Never Come Back. Which, of course, is just what you, wiser than we, have done in getting tattooed.

"Get out."

The ten plagues recorded as visited upon the Egyptians were, in truth, plagues upon the Jews. It was, psychoanalytically, they who were afflicted with Blood, Frogs, Hail, Vermin; they re-mained unmoved, until God wearied of their comfort in slavery and killed the firstborn, when they finally fled; and, yet, again they wanted to turn back—Pharaoh came after them, and God inter-posed before them, the Red Sea; Death behind and Death before, and that brought about the miracle of the exodus, and only that.

What was the miracle? That the Red Sea parted?

The Svas Emess taught that the parting of the sea was, to the creator of the universe, nothing at all. That was no miracle. The miracle was that the people went into the sea—and not until they walked into it, up to their noses, did it part. They did not go until they went in terror, and, once having gone, they were changed.

Eric Hoffer wrote in *The Ordeal of Change* that the greatness of America was that the immigrants had to undergo the or-deal. They had to leave their customs, their possessions, their language, and begin anew. Having done that, they found that they could accomplish anything.

They had escaped from the Comfort of the Known.

The possibility of change.

The Necessity of change.

We age, our body, our mind, our soul goes through trans-formations. The necessity of change will always feel intrusive, unpleasant, and dealing with it will always feel artificial, and unnecessary. That is why we have ritual.

On June 5, 1944, thousands of American paratroopers jumped into Normandy. Four men refused the jump. Can you imagine, can anyone imagine the rest of these men's lives? What prodigies of self-excuse, rationale, or repression they must have had to employ? Their lives, in effect, ended the moment they refused to leave the plane. As would the lives of the Jews, had they refused to go into the sea. As will yours and mine, and as they do in part, we each refuse the opportunity to change—we stagnate and perform ever greater prodigies of repression and hypocrisy, to explain to ourselves why we don't immerse ourselves in the mysteries of life. We all die in the end, but there's no reason to die in the middle.

You'll be, through your life, asked to renounce your petted excellences, your physical prowess, beauty, power, time—if you have children—and eventually you will have to renounce your life itself.

In addition to pain, these transitions offer, as they did to the paratroopers, the possibility of glory—not in accomplishment, but in surrender, as they bring one closer to a mystery.

What is this mystery?

A woman at my synagogue spoke up and said: Rabbi, I don't believe in God. The words were almost torn from her, and came out broken and anguished.

He said we have been told that God is a proposition. There is such a thing as propositional theology: God is: (pick all or some) good, bad, human, formless, male, female, sexless, vengeful, et cetera.

Various sects, various religions compile a list of propositions and state to their adherents: accept these, that is what it
means to believe in God, to believe in these propositions. But,
the Rabbi said, God is not a mass of propositions. God is unknowable. Why are we here, what formed the world, how will
it end, how can evil exist, what is sin, what is expected of all of
us, these are all part of a mystery—the desire to draw close to
the mystery is the belief in God. That is all it means.

Well. The mystery can't be lived with constantly. It presents itself to you, in admixtures, and at intervals. Sometimes
you look for it, and sometimes, it comes looking for you.
Sometimes the summons will be joyful and sometimes not.

Periods of self-sufficiency will be followed by periods of
doubt, of disbelief, as life changes around you, and, as part of
the mystery, periodically, change or die.

The journey from this summons to the next, unknowable
state must pass through ordeal, as the Jews at the Red Sea, as Christ
at the Cross, or Buddha at the Bo Tree. Perhaps, as you today.

The forces of parenthood, of education, are driving you
out and perhaps the world does not want you.

Today you are comfortably ensconced in an experience of
what you will later name as "childhood," and what is that dark
unknowable land before you?

It is good, it is bad, it is kind or cruel, pointless or tenden-
tious, whatever it is, it is legitimately for me and your parents and
teachers no less than for you, it is a mystery whose trials, and you
will discover, whose delights are beyond foreseeing.

Ask anyone up here if they would trade places with you,

and we might open our mouth to speak, with assurance, and then, whatever our answer was to be, say "I don't know."

Eric Hoffer wrote:

"No country is good for its juveniles. Like newly arrived immigrants the juveniles will adjust themselves to the status quo when they age given unlimited opportunities for successful action—for proving their adulthood."

It is as difficult for my generation to overcome its fear of the power of the young, to temper its reasonable assessment of your inabilities with a grateful concern for your development, as it is for your generation to control its ambition, and outrage at our inabilities, and corruption.

This passage, this graduation recapitulates, and, in fact, is a pagan ceremony, a return to the prehistoric ritual of two groups separated by a campfire. I wish that I could forge for you that ritual which would make your transition, not easier, but more final—you have already, many of you, taken that step, in getting yourselves tattooed.

Go further. Find a quiet moment. Take a drop of blood from your finger, press it to a sheet of paper. Set fire to the paper and watch it burn.

Perhaps that was your childhood. It's over now. You can't go back. Here is what my generation wishes you:

May the Lord bless you and keep you.

May the Lord lift up God's countenance to you and be gracious to you.

May the Lord cast God's light upon you and grant you peace.

FIDELITY, BRAVERY,
AND INTEGRITY

★

ROBERT MUELLER

College of William & Mary

CLASS OF 2013

ROBERT MUELLER was the sixth director of the
FBI under both George W. Bush and Barack Obama. He
served in the Vietnam War as an officer in the Marines.
Mueller was awarded two Navy Commendation Medals, the
Bronze Star, the Purple Heart, and the Vietnamese Cross
of Gallantry.

As I reflect upon where I have come since I myself
graduated, I will say that I never would have expected to end
up where I have. And I consider myself most fortunate to have
been given the opportunities I have had over the past thirty
years—both personally and professionally.

I have been blessed with three families: my family—my wife

and our two daughters; my Marine Corps family; and, for the past eleven years, my FBI family. And from each of these families, I have learned a number of life lessons. One such lesson is that much of what you do impacts those around you, and, in turn, those around you shape your life in a number of ways. Such lessons can often be frustrating as well as uplifting. Lord knows I myself have had plenty of opportunities to grow within these three families.

Today, I want to touch on three lessons learned through these relationships. These lessons relate to integrity, service, and patience—as well as its corollary, which is humility. Perhaps my experiences—and in some cases, my mistakes—will strike a chord with you.

I would like to begin with integrity because it is so essential to who and what you ultimately will become.

Many of you have a career path in mind. Many of you have no idea where you will end up. A few of you may be surprised by where life takes you. I certainly was. In the end, it is not only what we do, but how we do it. Whatever we do, we must act with honesty and with integrity.

Regardless of your chosen career, you are only as good as your word. You can be smart, aggressive, articulate, and indeed persuasive. But if you are not honest, your reputation will suffer. And once lost, a good reputation can never, ever be regained. As the saying goes, "If you have integrity, nothing else matters. And if you don't have integrity, nothing else matters."

The FBI's motto is Fidelity, Bravery, and Integrity. For the men and women of the Bureau, uncompromising integrity—both personal and institutional—is the core value.

That same integrity is a hallmark of this institution. William & Mary was the first college in the country to have a student-run Honor System. That Honor System, and the community of trust it enables, rests on one precept—and that is integrity. Your professional and your personal success will rest on that same precept.

There will come a time when you will be tested. You may find yourself standing alone, against those you thought were trusted colleagues. You may stand to lose what you have worked for. And the decision will not be an easy call.

But surely William & Mary has prepared you for just such a test. Indeed, your own Thomas Jefferson believed that William & Mary was "the finest school of manners and morals that ever existed in America." As graduates, you are charged with upholding this legacy of honesty and integrity. Today, you become the standard bearers.

Turning to the importance of public service, or service over self, I can say that I did not really choose public service. Rather, I more or less fell into it early on, perhaps not fully appreciating the challenges of such service. Yet one can come to understand the importance of service over self in a myriad of ways—through volunteerism, through commitment to a particular cause, or perhaps by example.

As an undergraduate, I had one of the finest role models I could have asked for in an upperclassman by the name of David Hackett. David was on our 1965 lacrosse team. He was not necessarily the best on the team, but he was a determined and a natural leader. He graduated later that spring. And a year later—as we were graduating—we faced the decision of how to respond to the war in Vietnam.

We knew that David was in Vietnam serving as a platoon commander in the Marine Corps. In the spring of 1967, he volunteered for a second tour of duty. But on April 29, as he led his men against a North Vietnamese Army contingent, David was killed by a sniper's bullet just south of the DMZ.

One would have thought that the life of a Marine, and David's death in Vietnam, would argue strongly against following in his footsteps. But many of us saw in him the person we wanted to be, even before his death. He was a leader and a role model on the fields of Princeton. He was a leader and a role model on the fields of battle as well. And a number of his friends and teammates joined the Marine Corps because of him, as did I.

I do consider myself fortunate to have survived my tour in Vietnam. There were many—men such as David Hackett—who did not. And perhaps because of that, I have always felt compelled to try to give back in some way. I have been lucky to spend the better part of my professional life in public service, and to benefit from the intangible rewards that come from such service.

The lessons I learned as a Marine have stayed with me for more than forty years. The value of teamwork, sacrifice, and discipline—life lessons I could not have learned in quite the same way elsewhere.

And when I look back on my career, I think of having the opportunity to participate in major investigations, such as the Pan Am 103 bombing over Lockerbie, Scotland . . . and working shoulder-to-shoulder with homicide detectives in Washington,

D.C. And I think of my experience over the past eleven years, working with one of the finest institutions in the world—the FBI. These were opportunities that would have been difficult to replicate in the private sector, and that, for me, has been time well spent.

Since its earliest days, the College of William & Mary has emphasized service over self. Your fellow alumni have served as the nation's highest political officers, attorneys and judges, teachers and doctors, and civic and military leaders.

The way in which you choose to serve does not matter— only that you work to better your country and your community. Each of you must determine in what way you can best serve others . . . a way that will leave you believing that your time has been time well spent.

Turning to lessons on patience.

Writer Barbara Johnson once defined patience as the ability to idle your motor when you feel like stripping your gears. For those of us who are not inherently patient—including myself—it is an acquired skill. And believe me, it is hard earned . . . and people will say that I am still learning. It is also fair to say that true patience is required at precisely the moment you least have time for it.

Patience includes the ability to listen—really listen—to others, and especially those close to you. This is not always easy, particularly for someone like me.

In one of my first positions with the Department of Justice, more than thirty years ago, I found myself head of the Criminal Division in the U.S. Attorney's Office in Boston. I soon realized that lawyers would come to my office for one of two reasons: either to "see or be seen" on the one hand, or to obtain a decision on some aspect of their work, on the other hand. I quickly fell into the habit of asking one question whenever someone walked in the door, and that question was: "What is the issue?"

A word of advice: This question is not conducive to married life.

One evening I came home to my wife, who had had a long day teaching and then coping with our two young daughters. She began to describe her day to me. After just a few moments, I interrupted, and rather peremptorily asked, "What is the issue?" The response, as I should have anticipated, was immediate. "I am your wife," she said. "I am not one of your attorneys. Do not ever ask me, 'What is the issue?' You will sit there and you will listen until I am finished." And, of course, I did just that.

That night, I did learn the importance of listening to those around you—truly listening—before making judgment, before taking action. I also learned to use that question sparingly, and never, ever with my wife.

Humility is closely related to patience. There are those who are naturally humble. But for others, humility may come from life experience; it is the result of facing challenges, making mistakes, and overcoming obstacles.

I would like to close with a story about one of your own— Lee Rawls. Lee was an adjunct professor here at William & Mary for more than eighteen years. He taught a seminar entitled "Congress, the Executive, and Public Policy." Lee was naturally humble. He was always the smartest person in the room, and the last one who would ever tout it.

Lee and I were college classmates, and we served together in a previous administration. When I became director of the FBI, I asked him to join me as a close adviser and remarkably, he agreed.

Lee knew how to cut through the nonsense and get to the heart of the matter better than anyone. He also knew how to put me in my place. During one particularly heated meeting, everyone was frustrated—mostly with me—and I myself may well have been a wee bit impatient and ill tempered. Lee sat silently, and then posed the following question out of the blue: "What is the difference between the director of the FBI and a four-year-old child?" The room grew hushed. Finally, he said, "Height."

On those days when we were under attack by the news media and being clobbered by Congress, when the attorney general was not at all happy with me, I would walk down to Lee's office, hoping for a sympathetic ear. I would ask, "How are we doing?" Lee would shake his head and say, "You're toast. You're dead meat. You're history." He would continue, "Don't take yourself too seriously, because no one else around here does."

It was that innate sense of humility—the idea that the world does not revolve around you—that was central to Lee's character. He never sought to elevate his own status; to the contrary, he sought to elevate those around him—the hallmark of the truly humble.

As you grow older, you will begin to understand that one's life is a combination of experiences and teachings of those who become your mentors. Lee Rawls certainly was a mentor to me, and I am a better person for having had the opportunity to be tutored by him. Though he might have suggested that it was rough going for him, having me as one of his students.

Lee passed away two years ago, and he is greatly missed by family, friends, and colleagues. His was a life of humility . . . a life of service; a model for many others—for you and for myself.

I encourage each of you to surround yourselves with such mentors over the coming years—individuals who will make you smarter and better, those who will recognize your potential and challenge you in new ways. And one day, wittingly or unwittingly, you will serve as a mentor to someone in your life. Remember . . . patience and humility. Both are hard to come by, and each will serve you well.

The lessons I speak of today are lessons not only for you, but for all of us. We must all find ways to contribute to something bigger than ourselves. We must cultivate patience, each and every day. We must maintain a sense of humility. And most important, we must never, ever sacrifice our integrity. If we do each of these things, we will have the best opportunity to be successful—personally and professionally—and our time will indeed have been time well spent.

Ten Simple Keys
to Failure

★

THEODORE OLSON

University of Georgia School of Law

Class of 2005

THEODORE OLSON is a lawyer and former solicitor general of the United States. Olson served as an attorney for George W. Bush during the Supreme Court case *Bush v. Gore*. He would later team up with David Boies, his counterpart on Al Gore's legal team, to successfully overturn Proposition 8 in California.

Knowing that I was going to be speaking to you today, a friend last Friday told me to relax; that it really didn't matter what I said. When he graduated from the United States Naval Academy some forty-five years ago, the speaker had been John Fitzgerald Kennedy. "Ted," he told me, "I don't remember a word he said. And if I don't remember John Kennedy's speech, surely no one is going to remembers yours."

So, I know that whatever I say is not going to be taken all that seriously, if noticed at all. Besides, I have been told that these days, graduation speakers should be "light and brief." And, if not "light and brief," at least "brief." Of course, that would constitute a break with the past. Graduation speeches historically have been long and ponderous to the point of intolerable. Think root canal.

It is also difficult to find anything to say at a graduation ritual that is not trite, sophomoric, pompous, boring, or all of these things at the same time.

As a result of these factors, I decided not to fill the air with hackneyed platitudes about how to succeed in life, or to be happy, rich, successful, and loved, or any of that overdone and sleep-inducing sentiment that has been dispensed at graduation ceremonies for centuries. You are all too bright and energetic to sit still or even stay awake very long for that sort of thing.

My solution today is to take the low road. At this moment in your lives, you have probably been saturated with idealistic advice about how to be a role model, model citizen, and super lawyer. But, I know something about law students at this point in the career path, and that is that a certain percentage of you are not remotely interested in remaking the planet into a better place. A few of you out there may actually want to squander the opportunities you have before you, disappoint your professors, and humiliate your family. That was certainly true in my law school graduating class. Some of my classmates seemed positively desperate to rush out there into the real world and sink like a stone. And they succeeded beyond their wildest expectations.

The few individuals in every law school graduating class who seem determined to fail manifest disturbingly similar characteristics: endowed with all the failure instincts and a will to overcome any bright opportunity for success. There can be no other explanation for some of the perversely counterproductive, socially unacceptable, and otherwise utterly inexplicable things that a few seemingly mature law school graduates do.

Just for the novelty of it, therefore, I thought that I would address the subject usually left unsaid in graduation ceremonies. Instead of talking about the high road to success, I will talk about the low road to failure and perdition. Consider this an extension of the equal time doctrine. Your soon-to-be-alma-mater has unwittingly set aside these few minutes for me to give you painfully frank counseling on going, not to the top, but to the depths. This is an interlude for the masochists among you; a brief journey, as it were, through the valley of the shadow of death.

Given my theme, I cannot very well be "brief and light," but I will at least try to be "brief and dark," so this will not take long. Cynics, pessimists, fatalists, curmudgeons, and naysayers are fast learners. You won't even have to take notes. And there will be no final exam. You won't need to study if you don't want to succeed. And, while there is much to say on this subject, I will try to be like those "how to succeed" books you see in the bookstores and on the bestseller lists and keep my presentation to ten simple keys to failure.

The first and most essential component for succeeding at failure is the appropriate mood and demeanor. This is easy if you have the aptitude for the attitude. Even for those who have stifled their darker instincts long enough to get good grades in law school, knowing how to fail is like riding a bicycle, it comes back easily. Here is how to do it: As H. L. Mencken advised, "when [you] smell flowers, look for the coffin." Learn to "read bitter lessons from the past; [be] prematurely disappointed in the future." Oscar Wilde suggested, for example, "when confronted with a choice between two evils, choose both."

Second, failure is like success, you may need help from others in getting to your goal: success at failure. You will find that you can enlist others in your enterprise without too much difficulty. For example, you can get others to despise you by adopting a smug and superior attitude. Make sure that everyone you meet knows immediately that you are a law school graduate, not someone to be trifled with. When you enter a room, behave as if everyone present should spring to their feet and cease all conversation. If you are a method actor, you can achieve this by imagining yourself as a federal judge, or perhaps the queen of England.

Or the legendary coach Vince Lombardi. When he climbed into bed one night after a bitter January practice in Green Bay, his wife said, "God, your feet are cold." Lombardi responded, "Dear, when we're here alone in bed, you can call me Vince."

Bear in mind that for the smugly superior person, it simply will not do to be impressed by the achievements of others. If you must profess admiration for anyone else's work, make it clear, as Ambrose Bierce put it, that you are simply "expressing polite recognition of [that other person's] resemblance to yourself."

There are several alternatives to the haughty, imperial, boorish, tyrannical, better-than-everyone style. One of them was once explained by the famous comedian and filmmaker Woody Allen. As a youngster, he worked at being as obsequious, sniveling, and unctuous as possible around anyone he thought could help him. He learned that nothing is better calculated to cultivate disrespect and loathing by everyone he encountered. Do this well and often enough, Woody found, and friends and neighbors, and even family members, will begin showing up on your doorstep with vats of boiling tar and bags of feathers.

Third, practice certain career-ending techniques to implement your planned self-destruction. I will mention just two.

One of these is to be a clone. Stifle your individuality. Surround yourself with people who look, think, and act just like you. Think of your life as a house of mirrors. Everywhere you look, you can see yourself. Think sheep. It is not a coincidence, by the way, that the first clone was a sheep. Who could tell that it was a clone? As one writer [Margo Kaufman] put it, "Don't be a sheep, people hate sheep. They eat sheep." But that is what you want. So if you can't be a clone, be a sheep. You've heard of a diploma referred to as a sheepskin. Take that literally, and wrap yourself in your diploma.

Alternatively, try carelessness, sloth, and indolence. As Eleanor Roosevelt explained, "no one can make you feel inferior without your consent." Here is how to give your consent: Just as attention to detail is universally perceived as a key to success, inattention to detail will pay immediate dividends in the opposite direction. Sign a letter with the name of your client, boss, or judge spelled wrong. Better yet, spell your own name wrong. Get dressed in the dark. Send e-mails without reading what you've typed or checking to see who you are really sending them to. Fill your vocabulary with unintelligible jargon. Talk to people as if they were idiots. Duck all hard assignments. As baseball great Ted Williams advised, "If you don't think too good, don't think too much." Show up at meetings late, or unprepared. Better yet, late and unprepared. And always have an elaborate and implausible excuse. Remember that successes, like promotions, babies, weddings, and even graduations, come with announcements. Failures announce themselves.

My fourth guideline for those who aspire to a dry, stultifying, unsuccessful career is to be risk-averse, and let everyone know it. As E. M. Forster said, "[It's better to] be a coward than brave because people hurt you when you are brave." So if you don't want to risk getting hurt, stay in the same job your entire life. Don't take on new challenges, or civic responsibilities. Don't write articles, give speeches, or teach. Don't get involved in politics or controversies. Stay below the radar screen. Wear gray clothes. Practice anonymity.

And don't experiment with government service. Everyone I have ever known who has spent at least some time working in government has come away richer in friendships, experience, and perspective. They became better, more versatile, more successful, and more productive as citizens. But that involves taking a chance, and thoughtful chance takers tend to wind up in those "who's who" books. That is not the career path we've been talking about. So, don't do any branching out. Think oak tree. Stay rooted in one place and watch as the world goes by.

By the way, risk-averse persons always swim with the current. You will soon realize that the only fish who swim that way, at least for very long, are dead. Sheep, lemmings, and dead fish all learn to head in the same direction at the same time. Be the kind of person who says, "There they go, I must hasten to follow them, for I am their leader."

While I am on the subject of risks and failure, I should say a word or two about experience. Experience is tricky because there are all kinds of experiences. It is the quality of one's experience that is important, and what we learn from what we experience is more important still. Some people seem never to learn that there are good and bad kinds of experience. One kind is the reason that insurance companies use the term "experience" to describe how many accidents someone has had. As one expert once explained, that is the kind of "experience that teaches you to recognize a mistake when you've made it again." "Good judgment," it is said, "comes from experience, and experience comes from bad judgment." If you want to fail, repeat the kinds of experiences that teach you that if you keep doing it the same way, you'll keep getting it the same way.

My fifth guidepost for you on your slide to failure is to be sure to set easily attainable objectives and standards for yourself. And avoid changing them. A few years ago, one of my law partners, frustrated with a professional setback, asked me, "When do I stop having to prove myself?" The answer, of course, is never. Not if you're going to continue growing, learning, and reaching loftier heights. A field goal kicker once explained, it's not that you are only as good as your last kick, you're only as good as your next kick. Watch what happens when you spend a lot of time marveling at your last accomplishment. When you look up, you will see that your competitors have been developing ways to beat you the next time. While you are patting yourself on the back, others will be tying your hands behind your back.

Success has a very short half-life, so, if you want to start down the path toward failure, you don't have to do much except to let up on the accelerator and start to coast. Failing to get better means getting worse. And, by the way, people will notice. You won't have to play any dirges for yourself. People will know right away when you start to die.

Six, listen only to people who agree with you or who will say what you want to hear. Since you are already smart enough, you won't be needing any advice or help from others. As Mark Twain explained, "Honest criticism is hard to take, particularly from a relative, friend, acquaintance or stranger."

The seventh lesson is to inflict gratuitous injury on those around you; your colleagues, friends, and family. And, find pleasure in the misfortunes of others. As Gore Vidal explained, "It is not enough to succeed, others must fail. Every time a friend succeeds," he said, "I die a little." For people like that, Ambrose Bierce commented, happiness is that "agreeable sensation [that arises] from contemplating the misery of others."

Be sure, by the way, to help your colleagues fall on their faces. Be discouraging, critical, and unimpressed. Put boulders in their paths, pebbles in their shoes, and grains of sand in their eyes. It is remarkable how thoroughly an organization can succeed if its members cheer on and help one another. It is equally amazing how swiftly an enterprise can be undermined, demoralized, and sabotaged by a few acts of selfishness, envy, or backbiting.

Feel free to acknowledge the deficiencies of your colleagues and the people for whom you work to outsiders, especially to journalists. You will be respected for your candor, your integrity, and your willingness to share your opinions with others.

This is especially good advice after something goes wrong, horribly wrong. After a disaster, you can point out that if others had only listened to you, or had been smart enough to "connect all the dots," as you obviously would have done, the catastrophe would never have occurred. Learn, and recite often, the phrase, "I told you so." This is a very valuable technique, because the retrospectascope is an inexpensive weapon and you can practice on Monday mornings after football games.

There will be plenty of opportunities to do this. Setbacks and unforeseen failures inevitably occur. And there are always others to blame. Let everyone know that "they" are responsible for your failures. By the way, you won't necessarily have to identify the culprits if you can't figure out who to blame. The pronoun "they" will generally do the job. Everyone will know what you mean: that dark conspiracy that is out there someplace foiling all your plans and ambitions. It will always be there for you. Remember the snowflake rule: "Every snowflake in an avalanche pleads not guilty."

The eighth tip for achieving a failed career is a corollary of the seventh. If it is impossible to blame others for a failure, accident, or scandal that has happened on your watch, you might consider either the reverse apology or the abstract, passive-voice apology. Both of these techniques are regularly practiced by politicians, and if a politician can learn them, you won't have much trouble learning how to do it. The first of these involves a statement of self-glorification masquerading as an apology. Former Washington, D.C., mayor Marion Barry used this technique after he was arrested for cocaine possession. He apologized for working so hard for the city that he fell prey to a narcotic addiction, thus adroitly blaming his irredeemably bad behavior on his essentially good character.

The passive-voice, abstract-tone apology is regularly employed by government officials, including presidents from Ronald Reagan to William Jefferson Clinton, to George W. Bush, when they can no longer avoid confronting a massive, odoriferous mess on their doorsteps. In these circumstances you will invariably hear some variation of the baleful acknowledgment that "mistakes were made." The official thus seems to concede that dreadful things have happened, but the passive voice removes the actor from the sentence, as if "mistakes" were unfortunate and pesky phenomena that simply show up like meteor showers. In the law we might call this nonliability without fault.

My ninth rule is a surefire technique that you regularly see with unsuccessful people. It is the overpromise, underdeliver gambit. This may take the form of résumé fraud, overstatements of past achievements, commitments to finish a project when it can't really be done on schedule, or promised results that won't be achieved. Successful people who deliver more than they have promised create satisfied customers, clients, colleagues, and even spouses. Unsuccessful people leave behind them a trail of frustrations at unfulfilled promises, the sound of gnashing teeth and bitter recriminations.

Finally, we reach rule number ten. At the end of the day, if all else fails, be angry. Anger is probably the most corrosive and therefore the most helpful emotion of all in stifling success. A flash of anger can in a heartbeat obliterate rational thought, good sense, morals, sound instincts, and a lifetime of good work. As Aldous Huxley taught, "Ye shall know the truth, and the truth shall make you mad." You've heard people say, "Get a life." Be the person they say that to.

Well, I promised to be brief. I hope that isn't one of those overpromises that I just mentioned. In this case, that would be underdelivered by virtue of being overdelivered.

The bad news for virtually all of you who wish to fail is that in your case, you will have to work hard to do so. You are talented, hardworking, and resourceful or you wouldn't be here today. And your friends, family, and colleagues want you to succeed. But perseverance, as William Faulkner explained in accepting his Nobel Prize for literature, is a potent force. Those who endure will prevail. And perseverance can get you nowhere just as surely as it can get you somewhere. If you're dumb enough to want it, you're smart enough to get it. For the rest of you, I tip my hat to you for the accomplishments that we celebrate today, and for the many in your future. This is one of those few moments in your life when you can pause, look back with pride at what you have achieved, and forward to a new passage in your life; a time when you can begin to open the doors that the degree you receive today have brought within your reach. Make the most of it and thank you for allowing me to celebrate your accomplishment and happiness with you.

FIND YOUR TALENT

★

BILL O'REILLY

Marist College

CLASS OF 2001

BILL O'REILLY is the host of *The O'Reilly Factor*, the most watched cable news program in the United States. He is also the author of eighteen books, including bestsellers *Killing Jesus*, *Killing Kennedy*, and *Killing Patton*. Here, he addresses students at his alma mater, Marist College.

Listen to me now. A few years after graduating from here I figured out something very important. I pinpointed the main talent that I was born with and it was the ability to write. Every person on this earth has a natural talent. You've got to find yours and then figure out a way to make a living using it. That's the key to happiness in your professional life. Don't let anybody else tell you what to do. You figure it out.

The reason I believe in God is because of this talent business. If there were no God, there would be a couple of slugs running into that wall over there. People who could not do anything. But that doesn't happen. Everybody can do something well.

Don't panic if you haven't figured out the talent thing. Take opportunities as they present themselves and work hard. Eventually, it will come to you.

Once you figure out your talent then you have to do the other very difficult thing in life. And that's to live honorably. You have to do what you say you are going to do. It's as simple as that. You don't have to read Descartes. You don't have to be a scholar. You simply do what you say you'll do all the time. If you live by that code you will accomplish what you want to accomplish.

The last thing I am going to tell you is this. There is an order to the Universe. The sun goes up, the sun goes down. The tide comes in, the tide goes out. The seasons change. There is also an order to your life. Good things are going to happen; bad things are going to happen. There is nothing you can do to prevent those things. But, it's how you react to the good and to the bad that will make the difference at the end of your life.

When you look back from your deathbed to what your life was, it all will come down to how you handled the things that came your way. How you evaluated people, how you chose your mate, how you chose your friends.

There is an order to your life. You will succeed unless you screw it up. Your parents and teachers have provided most of you with the opportunity to build a foundation. You can do what I have done. You can go beyond what I have done. Be honorable. Find your talent. Work hard. And be true to yourself. Your life is waiting for you.

Bad Advice for New Graduates

★

P. J. O'ROURKE

Change Magazine

May–June, 2008

P. J. O'ROURKE is an essayist and satirist known for his work in *National Lampoon, The Atlantic, The Weekly Standard,* and many more publications. He was the foreign affairs desk chief at *Rolling Stone* for many years, and is the author of twenty books, including *Holidays in Hell* and *Eat the Rich.*

Well, here you are at your college graduation. And I know what you're thinking: "Gimme the sheepskin and get me outta here!" Not so fast. First you have to listen to a commencement speech.

Don't moan. I'm not going to "pass the wisdom of one generation down to the next." I'm a member of the 1960s generation. We didn't have any wisdom.

We were the moron generation. We were the generation who believed we could stop the war in Vietnam by growing our hair long and dressing like circus clowns. We believed drugs would change everything—which they did, for John Belushi. We believed in free love. And the love was free, but we ended up paying a very high price for the sex.

My generation spoiled everything for you. It has always been the special prerogative of youth to look and act weird and shock the grown-ups. But my generation exhausted the earth's resources of weird. Weird clothes—we wore them. Weird beards—we grew them. Weird words and phrases—we said them. So, when it came your turn to look and act weird, you had to tattoo your faces and pierce your tongues.

Ouch. That must have hurt. I apologize.

True, my generation did have some good musicians. But those musicians are still out there touring. Therefore the only piece of good advice that I can give you is, don't start a rock band. You won't stand a chance against the Rolling Stones.

It's my job to give you advice. But all the rest of the advice I'm going to give you is bad advice. I figure it this way: You're finishing sixteen years of education, and you've had all the good advice you can stand. Let me offer some relief.

1. Go out and make a bunch of money!

Here we are in the most prosperous country in the world, surrounded by all the comforts, conveniences, and security that money can provide, yet no American political, intellectual, or cultural leader ever says to American young people, "Go out and make a bunch of money." They say money can't buy happiness. But it can rent it.

There's nothing the matter with honest moneymaking. Wealth is not a pizza where if I have too many slices you have to eat the Domino's box. In a free society, with the rule of law and property rights, no one loses when someone else gets rich.

2. Don't be an idealist!

Don't chain yourself to a redwood tree. Go be a corporate lawyer and make $500,000 a year. If you make $500,000 a year, no matter how much you try to cheat the IRS, you'll end up paying $100,000 in taxes— property taxes, sales taxes, excise taxes. That's $100,000 worth of schools and sewers, fire fighters and police. You'll be doing good for society. Does chaining yourself to a redwood tree do society $100,000 worth of good?

Idealists are also bullies. The idealist is saying, "I care more about the redwood trees than you do. Oh, I know you care. But you only care as much as you have to. I care and care and care. I care so much I can't eat, I can't sleep, it broke up my marriage. And because I care more than you do, I'm a better person than you are. And because I'm a better person than you are, I have the right to boss you around."

Get a pair of bolt-cutters and unleash that tree from the idealist.

Who does more to save the redwoods anyway—the person who's chained to a tree or the person who founds the "Green Travel Redwood Tree-Hug Tour Company" and makes a million by turning redwoods into a resource more valuable than backyard deck railings, a resource that people will pay hundreds of dollar just to go look at?

So get rich. Don't be an idealist. And . . .

3. Get politically uninvolved!

Politics stink—and not just bad politics. All politics stink. Even democracy stinks. Imagine if our clothes were selected by the majority of shoppers, which would be teenage girls. I'd be standing here with my midriff exposed. Imagine deciding what's for dinner by family secret ballot. I've got three kids and three dogs in my family. We'd be having Fruit Loops and rotten meat.

Think how we use the word "politics." Are "office politics" ever a good thing? When somebody "plays politics" to get a promotion, does he or she deserve it? When we call a coworker "a real politician," is that a compliment?

But let me make a distinction between politics and politicians. Some people are under the misapprehension that the problem is politicians—certain politicians who stink. Impeach George Bush, and everything will be fine. Nab Ted Kennedy on a DUI, and the nation's problems will be solved.

But the problem isn't politicians—it's politics. Politicians are chefs, some good, some bad. The problem isn't the cook. The problem is the food. Or let me restate that: The problem isn't the cook. The problem is the cookbook. The key ingredient of politics is the belief that all of society's ills can be cured politically. This is like a cookbook where the recipe for everything is to fry it. The fruit cocktail is fried. The soup is fried. The salad is fried. So is the ice cream and cake. The pinot noir is rolled in bread crumbs and dunked in the deep-fat fryer. This is no way to cook up public policy.

Politics is greasy. Politics is slippery. Politics can't tell the truth. But we can't blame the politicians for that. Because just think what the truth would sound like on the campaign stump, even a little bitty bit of truth:

"No, I can't fix public education. The problem isn't funding or teachers' unions or a lack of vouchers or an absence of computer equipment in the classrooms. The problem is your kids!"

4. Forget about fairness!

We all get confused about what role politics should play in life. This is because politics and life send contradictory messages.

Life sends us the message, "I'd better not be poor. I'd better get rich. I'd better make more money than other people." Meanwhile politics sends us the message, "Some people make more money than other people. Some people are rich and others are poor. We'd better close that 'income disparity gap.' It's so unfair!"

Well, I'm here to speak in favor of unfairness. I've got a ten-year-old at home. And she's always saying, "That's not fair." When she says that, I say, "Honey, you're cute. That's not fair. Your family is pretty well off. That's not fair. You were born in America. That's not fair. Darling, you had better pray to God that things don't start getting fair for you."

To heck with the income disparity gap. What we need is more income, even if it means a bigger gap.

5. Be a religious extremist!

So don't get involved with politics if you can help it, but if you can't help it, read the Bible for political advice—even if you're a Buddhist or an atheist or whatever. Using politics to create fairness is a sin. The Bible is very clear about this.

"Oh, gosh," you're thinking, "this is the worst advice yet. We get federal funding here. And the commencement speaker has just violated constitutional law about separation of church and state."

But hear me out. I am not, in fact, one of those people who believes that God is involved in politics. My attitude is: Observe politics in this country. Observe politics around the world. Observe politics down through history. Does it look like God's involved? No, that would be the Other Fellow who's the political activist.

However, in one sense I do get my politics from the Bible, specifically from the Tenth Commandment. The first nine Commandments concern theological principles and social law: Thou shalt not make graven images, steal, kill, et cetera. Fair enough. But then there's the Tenth: "Thou shalt not covet thy neighbor's house. Thou shalt not covet thy neighbor's wife, nor his manservant, nor his maidservant, nor his ox, nor his ass, nor anything that is thy neighbor's."

Here are God's basic rules about how we should live, a brief list of sacred obligations and solemn moral precepts. And right at the end of it is "Don't envy your buddy's cow." How did that make the top ten? Why would God, with just ten things to tell Moses, choose as one of them jealousy about livestock?

And yet think about how important this Commandment is to a community, to a nation, to a democracy. If you want a mule, if you want a pot roast, if you want a cleaning lady, don't whine about what the people across the street have. Go get your own.

So do get rich. Don't be an idealist. Stay out of politics. Forget about fairness. And I have another piece of advice:

6. Whenever you're unsure about what course to take in life, ask yourself, "What would France do?"

You see, France is a treasure to mankind. French ideas, French beliefs, and French actions form a sort of lodestone for humanity. Because a moral compass needle needs a butt end. Whatever direction France is pointing in—toward Nazi collaboration, communism, existentialism, Jerry Lewis movies, or President Sarkozy's personal life—you can go the other way with a clear conscience.

One last thing.

7. Don't listen to your elders!

After all, if the old person standing up here actually knew anything worth telling, he'd be charging you for it.

LOVE THE PEOPLE WHO
ARE CLOSEST TO YOU

★

RAND PAUL

University of Pikeville, Kentucky College of
Osteopathic Medicine

CLASS OF 2012

DR. RAND PAUL is the junior U.S. senator from
Kentucky and an ophthalmologist. He is the founder and
chairman of Kentucky Taxpayers United and the son of
former congressman Ron Paul.

I remember when my father went to medical school,
they used to say, "Look to your left, look to your right. One of
your classmates will not make it through medical school." By
the time I came to medical school, though, the adage had been
supplanted with the saying "Look to your left, look to your
right. One of your classmates will be married by the time you
finish school." We didn't complain. We thought, well, being

married sounded a lot less painful than flunking out of medical school.

I think today's version, though, is "Look to your left, look to your right. Both of your classmates will graduate with a mountain of debt." Graduation should, though, be about good news. So we won't dwell on the debt. Besides, you're going to hear plenty about the debt as the next few years unfold, not only with your personal debt, but your $45,000 share of the national debt. You will hear and see the results of a profligate nation. You will hear and see the ramifications of a spendthrift nation. You will hear a great deal and have plenty of time to assess blame to my generation, and to your parents' generation, for spending your inheritance.

Today, though, let us contemplate the brightness of your future. You have, today, achieved a special honor and distinction. As physicians, you will be accorded great respect in your communities, and among the population. For that distinction, you have studied and you have earned, and no one can take that from you. As a fellow physician, all I ask is that you are aware of the great privilege. You will be accorded the privilege to help patients. To overcome the ravages of disease. People who have worn out body parts, to help them to improve. The great satisfaction of destroying and sometimes defying cancer. You will inevitably witness, also, nature defeating modern medicine. You will witness the pain and suffering which sometimes defies explanation.

For some of you, becoming a physician may come easily. I doubt, though, if you are honest, that any of you will finish the path to becoming a physician without some degree of overcoming. For me, there's always been an element of overcoming. I'll never forget how my hand shook and my heart pounded the first time I drew blood. My first blood draw was from one of my best friends. I don't know if you still do it that way, but I had to draw from one of my best friends in medical school and he never lets me forget that it seemed like we were in San Francisco during a minor earthquake when I was trying to draw blood.

But with each subsequent draw, my courage and my steadiness improved until one day, a young man presented into the pediatric ER with burns over most of his body, and I volunteered to put in the subpalladium line, which was difficult, technically. The sense of accomplishment I felt in mastering a technique and using my hands to help someone survive can't be measured in concrete terms. And yet, years later when I performed my first corneal transplant on a rat in medical school, again my hands shook and my heart pounded. But in the end, not only could I perform corneal transplants on real patients, but I learned to do and transplant the very thin posterior portion of the cornea.

Now, did I ever experience failure? Absolutely. Did I quit? Did I say "I can't do this"? No. I overcame. Now, do I think I deserve a medal? No. But overcoming is normal, and I think every physician overcomes to one degree or another. When people say to me, "Oh, I could never be a physician, 'cause of my aversion to blood and guts and medicine," I reply that I think that it's normal, if not instinctual, not to like blood. To shy away from blood, or pain, or sickness; to become unaffected by death and disease isn't overcoming. But you will all experience it. But in that overcoming you all will have challenges. There is danger both in caring too much and in caring too little. Without doubt, all physicians create a bit of a wall around themselves to protect themselves from caring too much.

But in creating such a wall, you must be careful not to care too little. I practice in a fairly small town, as many of you will. You will see your patients in the grocery store and at church. I like that aspect of medicine; having people come up to you and thank you for helping them is priceless. It also helps to remind you that your task is not a cold and heartless technique, but an intimately human interaction that affects real people with real lives. It is hard though, sometimes, to care too much. I'll never forget my first patient on the surgery rotation. She had melanoma that had already spread to her ovaries. She didn't die during my rotation, but I knew her time was limited. How to explain such unfairness? She was a beautiful woman about my age at the time. How to explain her plight in a world that I believed must have some grand design?

Life is about overcoming. Overcoming our doubts, our fears, our own frailties. Politics is no different. When I gave my first speech, I was awful. I hope I'm better today, but I was awful. My hands shook and my heart pounded and I thought, "I can't do this." But, somehow, I did. Somehow, I became a better and more confident speaker. I know you're hoping the speech today will be good, but also succinct, and we don't delay getting to the after party. My point, though, is that very few of us are naturals at anything. For me, every aspect of my life has been an overcoming, or at least it appears so to me. Others say, "No, you had it made. Everything went your way." But assembled here, after four years of intense and rigorous work, you know that no one gave you this opportunity. You earned it. The question is, what will you do with it?

I'm a big believer in the big idea, that research, life, your marriage, your destiny should be based on the concept of the big idea. I think that, too often, medical research is missing the big picture. I think research is too bogged down in the minutiae to see the big picture. The trees may be microscopic, but they're still obscuring the view of the forest. When I was in medical school, my professors loved to talk about serendipity. That discoveries . . . come from observing a truth that occurs from being in the right place at the right time in discerning some truth that may or may not have been intentional. Some say Fleming, when he discovered penicillin, that he uncovered it. That he observed and had an "Aha" moment. An ordinary mold was inhibiting the growth of bacteria. Simple, but incredibly significant.

Will you be the one? Will you be the one who is open to serendipity? Will you be the one who is open to seeking the big question? For those of you going into research—search for the big idea. The big cure. The big answer. Don't get beaten down by the minutiae of the day-to-day life. Go big, go long. Don't let the everydayness of life sap your vision. Don't let the establishment squash your dreams. You are young. You are invincible. At least you think you are. Time may prove otherwise but, for now, shoot for the moon. Know no obstacles. The world is your oyster. Don't let them tell you it can't be done. Think outside the box. Be your own man or woman. Make a dent in life. Don't become part of the ebb and flow. Go out, find the cure for diabetes, the cure for cancer, the cure for heart disease. Go out and discover the reward that comes from treating and, perhaps, curing disease.

When I was a kid there was a sitcom on television called *The Beverly Hillbillies*. You've never heard of it because you have plenty of shows—we had three channels. That's all we had. But there was a little old woman, Granny, on there, and she had a great cure for the common cold. Her cure was a possum soup, and drink lots of fluids and wait two weeks. She was convinced she had this great breakthrough for modern medicine— the cure for the common cold. It may not have been, but you'll be surprised how often, as you encounter sick patients, that, really, the treatment they need is drink lots of fluid and wait two weeks. My wife chides me, she says, "They come to you and they pay good money and you tell them to put a hot compress on a sty." Well, in your practice, remember not to forget good old-fashioned and time-tested cures. Also remember not to forget that sometimes modern medicine can and should, at times, displace the best of homemade remedies. Know when to invoke the pharmacy and when to console and commiserate. When to apply a poultice is the art of good medicine. I would probably be still applying a poultice but I just don't know what a poultice is.

When I was young, I had great dreams. I wanted to cure diabetes. I wanted to experiment. I wanted to learn how to inject cells into the brain that would cure diabetes. My university wasn't involved in this and I somehow became involved in corneal transplants, and from that I became an eye surgeon. I didn't find the cure for diabetes. My career took a different path; I didn't find the answer. Many of you won't find the cure, either. I'm not saying don't begin the search, though. Please do. But whatever path you follow, remember not only to search for the big idea, but search for what are the important things. Success is measured in many ways. Ultimately, success is measured in man's humanity to man. I'm not asking you to love man in the abstract, I'm not asking you to love somebody else's neighbor. I'm asking you to love your own neighbor. I'm saying that what is important is to love the people who are closest to you.

Some may ask you to love man in the abstract. I think that's more difficult. I'm conscious of Pope's distaste for man in general. He presented the self-described misanthrope. But he didn't mean that he didn't like Tom, Dick, or Harry. Pope's misanthrope found it only possible to like man in the particular. Success or happiness or whatever you call it is in the particular. It's not in the abstract, it's sitting right next to you. Loving man or woman in the particular will help you to find happiness. Your interactions with those you know, with your patients, with those you love, is where you should look. In that realm, I believe, may lie the key to success, the key to happiness. Serendipity may be finding the secret among the banal. Maybe that secret is the same in science as it is in life. That secret may present itself before your very eyes if you just know where to look, if you know what to look for. For me, my serendipity, my discovery, happened not in the lab, not in medicine, not in politics. I didn't discover the cure for diabetes, but once upon a time I did serendipitously come upon a girl at an oyster restaurant. A girl who makes every achievement I might have or not have important. No matter where you are, what path you choose, don't lose track of what are the important things. The important things are the people—the people you know. The shared experiences of the ones you love. All that ultimately matters as you chart your course in your life is how you treat those closest to you. All else in life withers and fades.

Each of you will find your own path. Each of you will find what is important in your life. For me, it can be summed up in a dedication that I wrote in my book for my wife. In it I said, "What are the important things? Scratch my head, silence enough to hear my watch tick. Time. Have I time to even consider what are the important things? Even when I sit still, I sit still in a hurry. But beyond, between, and above all else, you, the girl, my wife, my love, can and do complete all the syllogisms my circular brain can create. For me, you are the important things."

What I wish for all of you is that you discover what in life, for you, are the important things. Thank you and congratulations.

WE HAVE SOMETHING WONDERFUL

★

MARILYNNE ROBINSON

College of the Holy Cross

CLASS OF 2011

MARILYNNE ROBINSON is a Pulitzer Prize–winning novelist. Her works include *Housekeeping*, *Gilead*, and *Home*.

I will tell you something you may not hear elsewhere. You live at a wonderful time in a wonderful country. I feel as strongly as anyone that everything could be much better, and ought to be better. But one of the pleasures of my self-defining life, my life as writer and teacher, is that I have read history, and I have traveled to and talked with people in those regions of America considered by many in this country to be alien territory. I have taken from history an awareness of the human tendency toward destructiveness and bitter violence. We share this tendency, certainly. But, in terms of our national life, we have cultivated an ethic of civil peace which has allowed for the flourishing of a great many wonderful communities and institutions. At the moment this ethic is under great stress, a fact that makes it all the more important to acknowledge it and recognize its value.

It is an honor to speak at an institution as distinguished as this one. But I am also honored to visit colleges I might never have heard of before they invited me. There are so many colleges and universities in this country—five thousand is the figure I have seen—many of them not in Massachusetts. However they might differ, they have certain things in common that are not common elsewhere. For instance, they tend to be beautiful, with grassy spaces and chapel bells and buildings that are meant to embody the serene gravity of the institution. Their students are local, or the children of graduates, or they are drawn to the school because of religious affiliation, but in any case they are as serious as students to be found elsewhere— not serious enough, that is, but as capable as any generation of assuming the role of adults in a complicated world. Or, to put it another way, they are as full of good faith, as imaginative and accomplished, as any generation that has lived before them. And they always feel well served by their teachers, as I believe they are.

It is generally acknowledged that most of the best higher education is to be had in the United States. At the same time we are constantly told that our high school graduates lag behind Brobdingnagia in every measurable skill. But, overwhelmingly, it is those same graduates who fill our colleges and universities, which could not sustain their high standards if the performance of their students were even relatively as abysmal as we are encouraged to believe. I deal constantly with a prejudice against themselves that is induced in young people by these invidious comparisons, often with student populations in other countries who have been winnowed at an early age, on the basis of competence or class, from a much larger population who do not receive academic education at a high school level. And these same countries make students specialize their training in math and science or language and humanities while they are still in high school.

So, with all due respect to the varieties of educational policy, the fact is that unlike things are being compared. We ought to be too sophisticated to base policy on this sort of thing. Clearly on this point our education has failed us. (And here I surrender parenthetically to the impulse to give a word of urgent advice. Think very hard about the meaningfulness of anything you are told, especially if it involves percentages or statistics. What I am really saying is, look very carefully at anything that would in any way disable the confidence you will need to make a full use of your judgment and your conscience.)

I go on about this because of that prejudice I mentioned. I work with young writers, in a program so selective that the yearly avalanche of applications comes near overwhelming us. Many of my writers have extremely handsome educational histories and broad experiences of the world. And many don't.

We choose our students solely on the basis of their writing. The rest does not interest us, since personal history is no predictor of distinction in the art we teach. The thing of interest here is that they are all equally persuaded that they are culturally or intellectually disadvantaged, relative to writers of other times and places. That is, they feel that culture and circumstance have relegated them to lesser levels of attainment. Big thought is not a thing they ought to attempt.

On one hand, modesty about one's education is wise and appropriate. At best it is an outline, an agenda, a curriculum for the decades of learning that should follow—and which, by the way, this big, buzzing civilization of ours has done an extraordinary amount to accommodate. And on the other hand, a modesty that disqualifies anyone from making a real, full test of his or her ability simply impoverishes the world. The attempt to take on ideas is full of perils, of course. Many people fear embarrassment. There are those who will not give words to a thought, in all silence and privacy, with a delete key at their fingertips, because they fear embarrassment. I see this so often in my teaching that I can only assume it affects many other disciplines as well.

This prejudice against ourselves has more important consequences, even, than the suppression of creative ambition. The American culture of education is under attack. Now people who are in some degree shaped by it are called an "elite," somehow alien, foreign occupiers on a terrain where learning is not native. In certain minds they are unsuited for participation in public life by evidence that they might, long ago, have been paying attention in class. This in a culture that has educated more people longer and at greater expense than any other country in history. It is not uncommon now to hear great public schools like mine spoken of as if they were burdens on the taxpayer rather than assets created by 150 years of investment by the people. We have something wonderful, and we should value it and make the best possible use of it, because it very much needs protecting.

Here is something I have learned from my travels. You can go almost anywhere in America and find an interesting cultural life. Big or small, all these campuses are in effect Chautauquas. They bring in poets and lecturers, they offer musical performances and stage plays. Often they are centers of study for local or indigenous culture, history, and environment. Often they are publishers of regional literature. They have interesting specializations, like geothermal technology and contemporary Central European music. It is surprisingly characteristic of any place in the country that people love it and are there for that reason. So their performances are local and their literatures are regional, and none of us has any reason to assume that they are not, therefore, of the first quality. This love of place is manifested in land and building preservation, the creation of archives, the revival of local culture and cuisine, in the development of new and traditional crafts, and in painting, poetry, and memoir.

A few weeks ago I went to a chamber concert, the debut performance of a newly commissioned work, in a gallery and performing arts center left to his small town by a local farmer. His cornfield was now restored prairie. The building was surrounded by experiments in sustainable agriculture. My first thought was that this was quintessential Iowa, and my second thought was, this could be anywhere in America, any well-loved place, with only the small differences of the things people choose to cherish. It would take the Census Bureau to estimate the number of reading groups there are out there. I would not hazard a guess at the number of novelists, or of shape-note singers, for that matter. Whatever may be wrong with us, we are not benumbed and television-besotted. Why all this good local life does not yield a more satisfactory national life I do not know. But it does suggest strongly that the lowest common denominator should be recalculated, that it should be a lot higher than it is now, and that we would be happier with our civilization if we had a better sense of it.

Of course it is hard to have a real sense of a country as big and busy as this one, and as heterogeneous. In the Middle West whole towns are effectively Norwegian or Dutch or German, Lutheran or Calvinist or Catholic. This is not the kind of diversity you see driving by, or flying over, but it is real and deeply felt. Frankly, this kind of focus on ethnicity makes me a little uneasy. Still, it is interesting in its own way. America is deeply inscribed by the history of the world, through its whole length and breadth.

But the inevitable difficulty in knowing the country is deepened by the ways we are encouraged to think that we do know it. Our generalizations are always uninformed and predictably unkind. Sometimes it seems to me that when we talk about Americans we forget we are talking about those irreducibly complicated creatures, human beings. I met a man in a prison in Iowa who had spent a stint in solitary confinement working on a villanelle. He could do this because student volunteers from Grinnell College come to the prison to teach. I met a woman in a prison in Idaho who said something to me I will never forget: Tell your students to write good books. They are all we live for. I visited a prison in Iowa where an inmate had asked the librarian to mark the books educated people would read. She had marked each one with a little square of green tape. We everywhere encounter amazing strangers. We have something to give them, and they have something to give us.

American colleges and universities are precincts meant to celebrate the life of thought. Why do we always assume they should be beautiful? Why all those meadows and gardens and walks and ponds? They are not islands in an intellectual desert, but expressions of a great consensus of belief, that education is not only valuable but also wonderful. You have enjoyed a strong education here on this beautiful hill, and now you are ready and able to enrich other lives as yours have been enriched, and to make this interesting country better and wiser. It needs you and it deserves you.

A few days ago I was at Oxford University, at the Rothermere American Institute, talking with British scholars and students about American history and politics. The experience was so striking that it made me revise the remarks I had prepared for today. These people at Oxford have every kind of information and experience relevant to the question of our national character. I grant the realities of cultural difference, which do not always sharpen insight into such matters. But if these same people had made negative comments about the country, I'd have felt obliged to take them seriously.

Instead they proposed some interesting theories, for example that, because ours is a religious culture, Americans are exceptionally inclined to take ethical positions and to assume responsibility for them. I think I am like most Americans in that I would love to believe these things are true, and yet I feel uneasy about taking them to be true. We know our faults so well. And we feel it is naïve at best to believe our country has special positive qualities, though we will grant that we have more than a few negative ones.

And modesty is a fine thing under all circumstances, except those in which it becomes disabling. What if it is actually true that the world looks to us for ethical insight, or to assume responsibilities that are compelling to us because of our religious beliefs? What if historical circumstance gives us a special role in the world, not in the sense that we should make any presumptuous claims, only that we should try to live up to the hopes others might have of us—by learning widely and thinking carefully, by disciplining ourselves toward fair-mindedness? The dominance of American culture in the contemporary world is lamented by some, and it can take unattractive forms. But as Americans we can try to ensure that it is a force for tolerance, reasonableness, and humane values.

There can be no question that the influence of this country is very great and that our responsibilities are therefore equally great. We can duck behind the notion that this influence is the work of great corporations and government agencies, and that we helplessly and innocently accept its consequences. But this influence is in fact very broadly cultural. As individuals we participate in the creation of it. After all, many of the greatest corporations are not American, and the religiousness for which we are apparently notable is not a trait of corporations, even those that are American.

To a very great extent we determine the nature of this influence—we, as individuals and communities. The work we do, the choices we make, the ways in which we educate ourselves and one another, the degree to which we live by our professed values, the care and deliberation with which we articulate our ideas and the willingness with which we say what we take to be true—these all go into the making of American influence.

It is easy to be disappointed, exasperated, with our religious culture, with blandness here and intemperance there, with fads and hypocrisies and a general failure to inculcate tradition. So it can come as a surprise to learn that on balance America gives religion a good name, that religion is associated through us with ethical seriousness among other things, and that its importance among us is considered by many to be enviable.

For those of us who are religious in any way or degree, the fact that much of the world, and certainly the secularized Western world, looks to us to see how religion is lived out, implies responsibility of a very high order. An institution like Holy Cross continues and exemplifies the unique historic importance of religion in the propagation of learning, and the love of learning, celebrated in the beauty and wealth of resources that typify American higher education. The association of religion with ignorance and narrowness is itself ignorant of religion's cultural importance, historically and at present, in humanizing and enlightening the whole of society.

As students here you have been given a deepened sense of thoughtfulness and good conscience, which are, as I have said, the most important things you can bring to the world. We are supposed to be a very practical culture, very solution-oriented, and yet we have a tendency to fret endlessly over things that can be fixed. If, like my students, you feel as though your very good education is incomplete, you can fix that. In your years here you have been taught how to learn. If you are wary of assuming responsibilities to which you might feel inadequate, make yourselves adequate. And here I refer again to the thoughtfulness and good conscience in which you have been instructed. If you feel that Catholicism or Christianity or religion is not represented, by detractors or defenders, in ways that honor its profundity and beauty, live out its profundity and beauty. To do this is more telling than any argument.

The truth should be faced and dealt with that in the contemporary world this country is exceptionally powerful and influential. Unless we accept this, we cannot be sufficient to our obligations. There is nothing historically exceptional in our situation. There are always two or three great powers in the world. We know the history that has made us great in this sense—notably the two world wars in which the powers of Europe inflicted and suffered devastation. If there are always a few profoundly influential countries, and one of them happens to have made a prolonged experiment in institutional democracy, wouldn't it be an excellent thing if that country made a good attempt at democracy? If its citizens really were loyal to the project, through all doubts and difficulties? If it was a nation composed of diverse cultures and populations, wouldn't it be an excellent thing if it acknowledged and enjoyed the ongoing renewal of continuing immigration? Wouldn't it be an excellent thing if such a country created marvelous resources for teaching and learning, and its citizens really became learned and informed and intelligently critical? And wouldn't it be an excellent thing if its great treasury of faith, with its thousand expressions, deepened and disciplined its citizens to make them honest and gracious stewards of the influence circumstance has given them? And, if we exclude the term "exceptional," and set aside concepts like "power" and "influence," would we not, in any case, be better and happier citizens of the world if we did these things? There is a great, democratic power in autonomous individual action and decision. By grace of the new technologies, this may be truer now than it has ever been before. Who you are, what you do, what you make of yourselves through learning, prayer, reflection, and service, all this will matter. Your lives are the life of this civilization, your hopes are its great hope.

There is a benediction we love in my church. Maybe you know it, too. "Go into the world in peace. Help the poor, heal the sick, support the faint-hearted. Return no one evil for evil, but in all things seek the good." There are many here more competent to bless you than I am, and they have blessed you in many ways. I simply offer you these words because they are excellent advice.

FREE ENTERPRISE, FAITH, AND THE COMMON GOOD

★

PAUL RYAN

Benedictine College

CLASS OF 2013

PAUL RYAN, a U.S. congressman from Wisconsin, was the Republican vice presidential candidate in 2012.

Whenever I'm in this type of situation, I usually ask myself, "What do I know now that I wish I knew then?" Well, life's not that easy. You can't just ask someone for the best shortcuts to take. You have to learn some lessons by living them. Those lessons tend to be the hardest—but also the most fulfilling. And often, they're lessons of faith. . . .

You know very well that faith isn't a Christmas ornament. It's not something you save for a special occasion. It's something you live with—and struggle with—every day. That's why it's so frustrating—and so comforting. It's always there. It's always waiting for you. Sometimes, the hardest part is simply finding your faith. It's finding out what you really believe. As you know, philosophy isn't a book of answers. It's a search for wisdom.

And my advice—in a nutshell—is to keep up the search. If you still have questions after four years of college—if you're not quite satisfied with the answers you have—discover for yourself what you really believe. Boil things down to basics. See how they add up. And if they don't add up, keep looking. That's why we call this a commencement because there's no end to your spiritual journey. As you gain in wisdom, you will more often make refinements to your views instead of big changes. And if you form your views this way—through discovery and debate, through deep thought and prayer—your moral code will be far more durable and rewarding.

But as you develop that code, you have to live up to it. You have to put it into practice. As Catholics, we're meant to be in the world, not of the world. We're meant to take up the vocation God has given us—and to do it well. Several years ago, I decided my vocation was public service. So today I want to talk to you about my faith—and my attempt to live up to it. I want to answer this question: How does a Catholic public servant apply Catholic social teaching?

There are different ways to answer this question. Today, I want to talk about two: our support for free enterprise and for strong communities. Now, good Catholics can disagree. And we do. That's the difficulty—and the beauty—of our faith. On some issues, the teaching is very clear. For instance, we must always protect the sanctity of life.

But on other issues, there's a broad arc of prudential judgment. And there's room for everybody. So I'm not going to stand here and vanquish some straw men erected for my position. I'm going to take on the straw men erected against my position. In short, I hope to make the moral case for free enterprise. In this effort, I speak only for myself. And I ask only for your consideration.

Like yours, my story of faith and understanding is personal—and far from complete. It began when my dad died. I was only sixteen, and it was tough on our family. It was tough on me. I'd been raised Catholic. I'd gone to Catholic school. I'd even served as an altar boy. I thought I had it all figured out. But when such a shock occurs in your life, it makes you question everything.

So at a young age, I started a lengthy search for answers. I read everything I could get my hands on: from Freud to C. S. Lewis, from Hegel to Hayek, from Aristotle to Aquinas—to everything in between.

In fact, you may have heard that I enjoyed the work of a certain female author whose books were monuments to the idea that men and women should be true to their individual passions—even in the face of relentless social pressure to conform. Yes, it's true. I was—and I remain—a huge fan of the *Twilight* saga.

After I was elected to Congress, I began to wrestle with many issues—both as a representative and as a Catholic. And as I wrestled with my views, I noticed two themes in my beliefs, both of which come from Catholic social teaching: solidarity and subsidiarity. They might sound a little intimidating. But they're actually quite simple.

Solidarity is the belief that we're all in this together. So we must be good to one another. We must be generous with our love—and withhold it from no one. And when we write the laws of our nation, we must never lose sight of our primary purpose: the common good.

Subsidiarity is like federalism. It's the belief that every part of our country adds to the whole. But for the whole to benefit, every part must be free to do its work—on its own terms. Yes, government must do some things. But it can't do everything. So it shouldn't assume other people's roles. And it shouldn't tell them how to do their work. The people closest to the problem are the most likely to solve it—because they know the community best.

We see this principle in the First Amendment. Religious communities do great things in our country. They care for the poor, the hungry, and the sick. And they do this work in their own unique way—guided by their conscience and their beliefs. That's why I strongly support measures to protect religious liberty. I believe Catholic institutions—like colleges, hospitals, and social agencies—should be free to do their work according to their moral standards. It's essential to our society. And it's essential to subsidiarity.

Over the years, we've been blessed to hear three popes make the case for these principles. Take John Paul II. He rallied the Polish people against the Soviet Union. He said, in effect, that communism was wrong. There was something beyond this world—and we knew it. There was a God—and we were his children. And by speaking the truth, he electrified the nation—thirty-six million strong—not with a promise of wealth, but with a simple call: "Do not be afraid!" He showed solidarity with the Polish people. And he freed them from fear.

Pope Benedict XVI warned us about another danger, which he called "the dictatorship of relativism." It's the belief that there is no right or wrong—that every person is a law unto herself. And it can't stand the truth—because the truth is self-confident and self-sustaining. So it snuffs it out. It burns books. It censors the press. But as St. Thomas Aquinas once wrote, "All men are forced to give their assent" to reason. Pope Benedict revived interest in his teachings. Just as his predecessor Pope John Paul freed Poland from fear, Pope Benedict taught us how to protect the world from falsehood.

These two popes showed solidarity with the oppressed. And today Pope Francis is showing solidarity with the poor—as the Church has done for two thousand years. He's breathing new life into the fight against poverty. He's renewing our commitment to help the least among us. He has a chance to lift the dialogue to a higher level. I hope he will heal the divisions between the so-called Catholic "left" and "right" so "that all may be one" in Christ—because it's the spiritually impoverished who need the most help.

Pope Francis calls "the tyranny of relativism" "the spiritual poverty of our time." And it afflicts rich countries worst of all, including our own. To truly help the poor, we have to help the "whole" person, not just the material needs, but the spiritual ones too. The fact is, government can't give this help because the law is blind. It treats everyone the same. And though we're all equal, we're not all the same. We have different needs.

Only people can meet these needs. And though most people who serve in government are hardworking, they can do only so much. They can't give us the personal attention we need. So we need to look for people outside of government. And we will find them in our communities—in our churches and schools, in our nonprofits and neighborhoods, in our friends and families. Academics like to call these things "mediating institutions." But in the end, they're just people—people working together.

And government must not push them out. It must not crowd out society. Instead, it must support them. It must allow these groups to address our needs. It must expand the space for society. And one of the best examples of such a partnership is the free enterprise system.

Free enterprise is an example of that second principle: subsidiarity. It allows each person to contribute to society. It allows them to discover their talents and to pursue their dreams because when they do, they add to the common good. They create jobs. They save lives. They feed people. They add to the store of knowledge. And most important, free enterprise gives us the resources to care for ourselves and for others. It helps to ease human suffering.

We know the power of free people working together. We see it most clearly when it's absent. I want to borrow an example from Father Robert Sirico. Look at a picture of the world at night. You'll see light across the globe. One exception is in the northern half of the Korean peninsula. In North Korea, there's only one point of light—in Pyongyang, the capital, where the elite live. There's no free enterprise in the country. People aren't allowed to buy or sell, to trade or bargain, to build or create. And they suffer because of it. They're trapped in darkness.

So why is there such resistance to free enterprise? It's the old problem of greed. The critics say nothing good comes from commerce. They think it's all pinstripes and no principle. Sure, free enterprise makes more stuff, they argue. But it relies on "greed"—on people pursuing their self-interest. And isn't the love of money the root of all evil . . . or something to that effect?

Look, many people want the chance to get ahead. And to get ahead in a free economy, they must serve the needs of society. At some level, we all ask ourselves, How can I make ends meet? But the successful ask a better question: What's something people need? Voluntary exchange is an act of good faith. It gives the buyer a good in exchange for something of equal value. It creates a culture of personal responsibility and goodwill. To attract customers, you must be trustworthy. To attract workers, you must treat them with dignity.

Free enterprise helps the workers themselves because work gives people more than a paycheck. It gives them a sense of pride—a sense of purpose. It makes them a part of their communities. And when we share our gifts with other people, we show solidarity with each other. If farmers didn't harvest, people would go hungry. If doctors and nurses didn't practice, the sick would go untreated. We don't think of ourselves as greedy—even though we take part in the economy. And we shouldn't because we're working to help our families. We're helping to put food on the table, to pay for our education, to save for retirement.

Yes, we must guard against greed. But greed will always be with us. Our job is to limit its power. Free enterprise doesn't reward greed. It rewards value because competition checks greed. And there's no greater opportunity for greed than government cronyism. Greed knows how to exploit the pages of regulations. It knows how to navigate the halls of power. So if we're concerned about greed, we shouldn't give it more opportunities to grow.

No, money isn't everything. Wealth is a means to an end. And the end isn't a full bank account. The end is a good life— one lived in accordance with God. And to live a truly good life, we must go beyond ourselves. We must minister to the poor and the sick. We can't outsource the job. Concern for the poor doesn't demand faith in big government. It demands something more—from all of us.

If we continue to believe that the war on poverty is primarily a government responsibility, then we will continue to weaken our communities. We will drift further apart as people.

As Catholics, we know happiness can't be bought or sold. And it can't be legislated. Earning your just rewards from achievement and hard work promotes human flourishing and happiness. It brings fulfillment both to yourself and to others. In short, we find happiness only in the thrill of accomplishment, in the comfort of community, and in communion with God. This is how solidarity and subsidiarity work together: They create a society that serves the poor. They create healthy communities by building healthy relationships. And on this philosophy—from this beachhead—we can fight back the growth of relativism.

That's my take on Catholic social teaching. As you can see,

it's not a step-by-step guide. It's a philosophy. It grounds you in certain principles. In a culture that stresses the "I," the Church stresses the "we." In a culture that liberates the passions, the Church shows that discipline gives you freedom. And in a world where relativism threatens the weak, the Church works to protect the poor and the powerless. These are the truths that anchor Catholic social teaching. They offer guidance as you discover God's plan for you.

Your task is to consider that guidance as you continue your search for wisdom. This is the advice I plan on giving my children. Naturally, I hope they take up my own point of view. Most parents feel that way. But you can't be secure in your beliefs until you know how they stack up against others'. So my advice is to keep searching—to keep questioning. And when you need a port of call, I hope you will take comfort in the Church, as I have. And when you do, you will know for certain that you're there to stay.

Our Catholic faith has endured for thousands of years—and for a reason. The world offers many challenges. Our legacy will endure if you can handle those challenges. Here, at Benedictine, you are off to a great start. I wish you continued success as you find your path. And whether you walk on the left side of the street or the right, whether you walk the straight and narrow—or you take the scenic route—I hope you will always walk with God.

TRADE-OFFS

★

THOMAS SARGENT

University of California, Berkeley

CLASS OF 2007

THOMAS SARGENT is a Nobel Prize–winning economist. His speech to graduates at Berkeley is widely celebrated as a masterpiece of clarity and brevity.

I remember how happy I felt when I graduated from Berkeley many years ago. But I thought the graduation speeches were long. I will economize on words.

Economics is organized common sense. Here is a short list of valuable lessons that our beautiful subject teaches.

1. Many things that are desirable are not feasible.

2. Individuals and communities face trade-offs.

3. Other people have more information about their abilities, their efforts, and their preferences than you do.

4. Everyone responds to incentives, including people you want to help. That is why social safety nets don't always end up working as intended.

5. There are trade-offs between equality and efficiency.

6. In an equilibrium of a game or an economy, people are satisfied with their choices. That is why it is difficult for well-meaning outsiders to change things for better or worse.

7. In the future, you too will respond to incentives. That is why there are some promises that you'd like to make but can't. No one will believe those promises because they know that later it will not be in your interest to deliver. The lesson here is this: Before you make a promise, think about whether you will want to keep it if and when your circumstances change. This is how you earn a reputation.

8. Governments and voters respond to incentives too. That is why governments sometimes default on loans and other promises that they have made.

9. It is feasible for one generation to shift costs to subsequent ones. That is what national government debts and the U.S. social security system do (but not the social security system of Singapore).

10. When a government spends, its citizens eventually pay, either today or tomorrow, either through explicit taxes or implicit ones like inflation.

11. Most people want other people to pay for public goods and government transfers (especially transfers to themselves).

12. Because market prices aggregate traders' information, it is difficult to forecast stock prices and interest rates and exchange rates.

EXAMINE THE PLATITUDES

★

ANTONIN SCALIA

Langley High School

CLASS OF 2010

JUSTICE ANTONIN SCALIA has been a justice of the U.S. Supreme Court since 1986. The following is an excerpt from his speech at Langley High School, a public high school in Virginia.

Today, to be sure, we have the capacity to destroy the entire world with the bomb. I suppose you could consider that a new problem, but it is really new in degree, rather than in kind. If you were a teenager graduating from the Priam Memorial High School in Troy about 1500 B.C., with an army of warlike Greeks camped all around the city walls, and if you knew that losing the war would mean—as it did—that the city would be utterly destroyed, its men killed, its women and children sold into slavery, I doubt that that prospect was any less

209

terrible to you than the prospect of the destruction of the world. It was all the world you ever used anyway. Your country, your family, your friends, your entire society. The thought that other societies, at least, would go on was probably of no more comfort to the Trojans, or later to the Carthaginians, who were also utterly destroyed, or to the Campbell clan, which was massacred at Glencoe, than it is of comfort to you, that if this world is incinerated, well, it's good to know there may be others.

The challenges faced by different societies at different times take different forms. Defending against the longbow, versus defending against the S4 missile—but in substance, they are always the same. Number one, the forces of nature: how do we assure our continuing supply of clean air and water, food, fuel, shelter, and clothing? And number two, the forces of man: how to get along with one another, or defend against those we cannot get along with.

It is important that you not believe you face unprecedented challenges, not only because you might get discouraged, but also because you might come to think that the lessons of the past, the wisdom of humanity—those are a couple of good platitudes—which it is the purpose of education to convey, is of not much use. I occasionally give a little talk about the Constitution, in the course of which I discuss some of the writings of the founding fathers in *The Federalist Papers*. They knew they were facing a great challenge in seeking to establish, in one at the same time, a new federation and a democracy. They did not think for a moment it was an unprecedented challenge. If you read *The Federalist Papers*, you will find that they are full of examples to support particular dispositions in the Constitution. Examples from Greece, from Rome, from medieval Italy, from France and Spain. So if you want to think yourselves educated, do not think that you face unprecedented challenges.

Much closer to the truth is a quite different platitude: there's nothing new under the sun.

The second platitude I want to discuss comes in many flavors. It can be variously delivered as "Follow your star," or "Never compromise your principles." Or, quoting Polonius in *Hamlet*—who people forget was supposed to be an idiot—"To thine own self be true." Now this can be very good or very bad advice. Indeed, follow your star if you want to head north and it's the North Star. But if you want to head north and it's Mars, you had better follow somebody else's star.

Indeed, never compromise your principles. Unless, of course, your principles are Adolf Hitler's. In which case, you would be well advised to compromise your principles, as much as you can. And indeed, to thine own self be true, depending upon who you think you are.

It's a belief that seems particularly to beset modern society, that believing deeply in something, and following that belief, is the most important thing a person could do. Get out there and picket, or boycott, or electioneer, or whatever. Show yourself to be a committed person, that's the fashionable phrase. I am here to tell you that it is much less important how committed you are, than what you are committed to. If I had to choose, I would always take the less dynamic, indeed even the lazy person who knows what's right, than the zealot in the cause of error. He may move slower, but he's headed in the right direction.

Movement is not necessarily progress. More important than your obligation to follow your conscience, or at least prior to it, is your obligation to form your conscience correctly. Nobody— remember this—neither Hitler, nor Lenin, nor any despot you could name, ever came forward with a proposal that read, "Now, let's create a really oppressive and evil society." Hitler said, let's take the means necessary to restore our national pride and civic order. And Lenin said, let's take the means necessary to assure a fair distribution of the goods of the world. In short, it is your responsibility, men and women of the Class of 2010, not just to be zealous in the pursuit of your ideals, but to be sure that your ideals are the right ones. Not merely in their ends, but in their means. That is perhaps the hardest part of being a good human being: good intentions are not enough. Being a good person begins with being a wise person, then when you follow your conscience, will you be headed in the right direction.

The next platitude I want to address is perhaps the most common one, especially at graduation addresses, and most especially at graduations in the Washington area. I refer to the phrase "The United States is the greatest country in the world." Now, I do not intend to contradict that platitude, because I think it to be true. What I would like to explore with you a little bit is, what it is we mean when we say we believe it.

A few possible things could be easily rejected. We don't mean, certainly, the most physically beautiful country in the world. Acre-for-acre, Switzerland has it all over us. Even if you take the total number of scenic wonders, I'm not sure we would come out first, at least you couldn't be sure unless you traveled everywhere.

Nor do we mean, by the greatest country, the most powerful country. Because then, we would have to think that next to living in the United States, we would like to live in China or Russia, which I doubt is the case.

Perhaps then what we mean when we say our country is the greatest is that it best satisfies both the physical and spiritual desires of its people. But no, we couldn't mean that, because on that analysis the nation of Attila the Hun could be considered great. It certainly satisfied the physical desire of its people—to take everything in sight—and the principled spiritual desire of its people—to dominate others.

Perhaps then we think it to be the greatest because it is the freest. Now there is a real possibility. In fact, I think that is the platitude derivative of the one I am now discussing; mainly, we are the greatest because we are the freest. I've heard that very often, as I suppose you have. But is it really true? If so, then I suppose the really greatest nation in the world would be the one where there were no laws, where chaos prevailed. The Wild West, perhaps, in the days before the law arrived, when a fellow could shoot up a town unless somebody bigger could stop him. No, that can't be the answer either.

Not to keep you in suspense, let me tell you what I think the answer is. We are the greatest because of the good qualities of our people. And because of the governmental system that gives room for those qualities to develop. I refer to qualities such as generosity. Americans are there not only when their neighbors need help, but even when strangers on the other side of the world do. Qualities such as honesty. Americans are by and large people you can trust. George Washington and the cherry tree, Abe Lincoln returning the book in the snowstorm, are part of our national tradition. Qualities such as constancy. Americans can be counted on. They're not quitters, even when things look bleak. Valley Forge and Bull Run are part of our tradition, too. Qualities such as tolerance. Americans believe in things, and believe deeply. But they'll try to persuade others to their way of thinking, and not coerce them. The First Amendment, and the Virginia declaration of religious freedom, are part of our national tradition, too. And I could go on; self-reliance, initiative, civility—these are also qualities we take pride in and regard as especially American, characteristic of our great country. These are what make us the greatest.

The point I'm driving toward, and maybe it's taking me too long to get there, is that not only is it not true that we are the greatest because we are the freest, rather precisely the opposite is true: we are the freest because we have those qualities that make us the greatest. For freedom is a luxury that can be afforded only by the good society. When civic virtue diminishes, freedom will inevitably diminish as well.

Take the simplest example. Many municipalities do not have any ordinances against spitting gum out on the sidewalk. As far as the law is concerned, you are free to do that. But that freedom is a consequence of the fact that not many people are so thoughtless as to engage in that practice. And if that behavior becomes commonplace, you can be absolutely sure that an ordinance will be passed, and the freedom will disappear.

The same principle applies in larger matters. The English legal philosopher Lord Acton had it right when he said, "That society is the freest, which is the most responsible." The reason is quite simple and inexorable, legal constraint—the opposite of freedom—is in most of its manifestations a cure for irresponsibility. You are familiar with Madison's famous passage in No. 51 of *The Federalist Papers*, "What is government itself but the greatest reflection upon human nature? If men were angels, no government would be necessary." The same can be true of the product of government, which is laws, and the constraints upon individuals which those laws establish. Law steps in, and will inevitably step in, when the virtue of the society itself is inadequate to produce the needed result. When the society is composed entirely of criminals, only the strict regimentation of a prison will suffice.

If I am right that we are the freest because we are the greatest, the message for your lives should be clear: do not go about praising the Bill of Rights and the wonderful liberties we enjoy without at the same time developing within you, yourselves, and within those whose lives you touch, the virtue that makes all that possible.

The last platitude I want to mention is appropriately last, because it usually comes toward the end of a commencement address, and goes somewhat like this: "Graduates, this is not an end, it is a beginning." I want to tell you that is not true. There is no more sudden end, no more significant rite of passage in our society, no more abrupt termination of a distinct age of your life than the graduation from high school and the departure from home that soon follows.

You have been living up to now in the moral environment that could be closely supervised by the people who love you most in the world, your parents. They got to know your friends, your teachers, your school, and did what they could to change or improve them, when they thought that was for your own good. Most of you will be going off to college, which is not a place where your parents can control the influences upon your character, and which is not, by and large, a place where anybody serves to exercise that control as well.

From here on out, you are much more than you have ever been—I'm hoping for a platitude to convey the thought—captains of your own ship. Masters of your own destiny. Your moral formation, what makes you a good person, or a bad one, a success in all that matters, or a failure, is now very much up to you. As a parent who has sent off nine children from high school, away from home, and into a world that has a lot of wisdom, but also a lot of folly, a lot of good, but also a lot of bad, I assure you that if you are not at all worried about the prospect, your parents are.

But there comes a time to let go. And that is now. I have high hopes for the Langley Class of 2010, because I know some of them, I know some of their teachers, and I know the quality of education in knowledge as well as in goodness that Langley has provided. Good luck, and let's see, I had one last platitude I was going to—oh, yes: the future is in your hands.

Bingo.

THE REAL PUBLIC SERVICE

★

THOMAS SOWELL

June 2010

THOMAS SOWELL is an economist, a writer, and a social commentator. He is currently a senior fellow at the Hoover Institution at Stanford University. Sowell is the author of such books as *Black Rednecks and White Liberals* and *Intellectuals and Society*. The following is an excerpt from his syndicated column.

Every year about this time, big-government liberals stand up in front of college commencement crowds across the country and urge the graduates to do the noblest thing possible—become big-government liberals.

That isn't how they phrase it, of course. Commencement speakers express great reverence for "public service," as distinguished from narrow private "greed." There is usually not the slightest sign of embarrassment at this self-serving celebration of the kinds of careers they have chosen—over and above the careers of others who merely provide us with the food we eat, the homes we live in, the clothes we wear, and the medical care that saves our health and our lives.

What I would like to see is someone with the guts to tell those students: Do you want to be of some use and service to your fellow human beings? Then let your fellow human beings tell you what they want—not with words, but by putting their money where their mouth is.

You want to see more people have better housing? Build it! Become a builder or developer—if you can stand the sneers and disdain of your classmates and professors who regard the very words as repulsive.

Would you like to see more things become more affordable to more people? Then figure out more efficient ways of producing things or more efficient ways of getting those things from the producers to the consumers at a lower cost.

That's what a man named Sam Walton did when he created Wal-Mart, a boon to people with modest incomes and a bane to the elite intelligentsia. In the process, Sam Walton became rich. Was that the "greed" that you have heard your classmates and professors denounce so smugly? If so, it has been such "greed" that has repeatedly brought prices down and thereby brought the American standard of living up.

Back at the beginning of the twentieth century, only 15 percent of American families had a flush toilet. Not quite one fourth had running water. Only 3 percent had electricity and 1 percent had central heating. Only one American family in a hundred owned an automobile.

By 1970, the vast majority of those American families who were living in poverty had flush toilets, running water, and electricity. By the end of the twentieth century, more Americans were connected to the Internet than were connected to a water pipe or a sewage line at the beginning of the century.

More families have air-conditioning today than had electricity then. Today, more than half of all families with incomes below the official poverty line own a car or truck and have a microwave.

This didn't come about because of the politicians, bureaucrats, activists, or others in "public service" that you are supposed to admire. No nation ever protested its way from poverty to prosperity or got there through rhetoric or bureaucracies.

It was Thomas Edison who brought us electricity, not the Sierra Club. It was the Wright brothers who got us off the ground, not the Federal Aviation Administration. It was Henry Ford who ended the isolation of millions of Americans by making the automobile affordable, not Ralph Nader.

Those who have helped the poor the most have not been those who have gone around loudly expressing "compassion" for the poor, but those who found ways to make industry more productive and distribution more efficient, so that the poor of today can afford things that the affluent of yesterday could only dream about.

The wonderful places where you are supposed to go to do "public service" are as sheltered from the brutal test of reality as you have been on this campus for the last four—or is it six?—years. In these little cocoons, all that matters is how well

LETTERS TO GRADUATES

★

BRET STEPHENS

Previously published in *The Wall Street Journal*

MAY 9, 2012, AND MAY 19, 2014

BRET STEPHENS is a Pulitzer Prize–winning journalist and author of *America in Retreat: The New Isolationism and the Coming Global Disorder*. He served as the editor in chief of *The Jerusalem Post*. The following are two commencement speeches not delivered, but rather published in *The Wall Street Journal* in 2012 and 2014.

Dear Class of 2012:

Allow me to be the first one not to congratulate you. Through exertions that—let's be honest—were probably less than heroic, most of you have spent the last few years getting inflated grades in useless subjects in order to obtain a debased degree. Now you're entering a lousy economy, courtesy of the very president whom you, as freshmen, voted for with such enthusiasm. Please spare us the self-pity about how tough it is to look for a job while living with your parents. They're the ones who spent a fortune on your education only to get you back—return-to-sender, forwarding address unknown.

No doubt some of you have overcome real hardships or taken real degrees. A couple of years ago I hired a summer intern from West Point. She came to the office directly from weeks of field exercises in which she kept a bulletproof vest on at all times, even while sleeping. She writes brilliantly and is as self-effacing as she is accomplished. Now she's in Afghanistan fighting the Taliban.

If you're like that intern, please feel free to feel sorry for yourself. Just remember she doesn't.

Unfortunately, dear graduates, chances are you're nothing like her. And since you're no longer children, at least officially, it's time someone tells you the facts of life. The other facts.

Fact One is that, in our "knowledge-based" economy, knowledge counts. Yet here you are, probably the least knowledgeable graduating class in history.

A few months ago, I interviewed a young man with an astonishingly high GPA from an Ivy League university and aspirations to write about Middle East politics. We got on the subject of the Suez Crisis of 1956. He was vaguely familiar with it. But he didn't know who was president of the United States in 1956. And he didn't know who succeeded that president.

Pop quiz, Class of '12: Do you?

Many of you have been reared on the cliché that the purpose of education isn't to stuff your head with facts but to teach you how to think. Wrong. I routinely interview college students, mostly from top schools, and I notice that their brains are like old maps, with lots of blank spaces for the uncharted terrain. It's not that they lack for motivation or IQ. It's that they can't connect the dots when they don't know where the dots are in the first place.

Now to Fact Two: Your competition is global. Shape up. Don't end your days like a man I met a few weeks ago in Florida, complaining that Richard Nixon had caused his New York City business to fail by opening up China.

In places like Ireland, France, India, and Spain, your most talented and ambitious peers are graduating into economies even more depressed than America's. Unlike you, they probably speak several languages. They may also have a degree in a hard science or engineering—skills that transfer easily to the more remunerative jobs in investment banks or global consultancies.

I know a lot of people like this from my neighborhood in New York City, and it's a good thing they're so well mannered because otherwise they'd be eating our lunch. But if things continue as they are, they might soon be eating yours.

Which reminds me of Fact Three: Your prospective employers can smell BS from miles away. And most of you don't even know how badly you stink.

When did puffery become the American way? Probably around the time Norman Mailer came out with *Advertisements for Myself.* But at least that was in the service of provoking an establishment that liked to cultivate an ideal of emotional restraint and public reserve.

To read through your CVs, dear graduates, is to be assaulted by endless Advertisements for Myself. Here you are, twenty-one or twenty-two years old, claiming to have accomplished feats in past summer internships or at your school newspaper that would be hard to credit in a biography of Walter Lippmann or Ernie Pyle.

If you're not too bright, you may think this kind of nonsense goes undetected; if you're a little brighter, you probably figure everyone does it so you must as well.

But the best of you don't do this kind of thing at all. You have an innate sense of modesty. You're confident that your résumé needs no embellishment. You understand that less is more.

In other words, you're probably capable of thinking for yourself. And here's Fact Four: There will always be a market for people who can do that.

In every generation there's a strong tendency for everyone to think like everyone else. But your generation has an especially bad case, because your mass conformism is masked by the appearance of mass nonconformism. It's a point I learned from my West Point intern, when I asked her what it was like to lead such a uniformed existence.

Her answer stayed with me: wearing a uniform, she said, helped her figure out what it was that really distinguished her as an individual.

Now she's a second lieutenant, leading a life of meaning and honor, figuring out how to Think Different for the sake of a cause that counts. Not many of you will be able to follow in her precise footsteps, nor do you need to do so. But if you can just manage to tone down your egos, shape up your minds, and think unfashionable thoughts, you just might be able to do something worthy with your lives. And even get a job. Good luck!

★

Dear Class of 2014:

Allow me to be the first to offend you, baldly and unapologetically. Here you are, twenty-two or so years on planet Earth, and your entire lives have been one long episode of offense-avoidance. This spotless record has now culminated in your refusals to listen to commencement speakers whose mature convictions and experiences might offend your convictions and experiences, or what passes for them.

Modern education has done its work well: in you, Class of 2014, the coward soul has filled the void left by the blank mind.

When I last delivered a commencement address via column to the Class of 2012, I complained about the dismaying inverse relationship between that class's self-regard and its command of basic facts. This led to one cascade of angry letters, blog posts, and college newspaper columns from the under-twenty-five set—and another cascade of appreciative letters from their parents, professors, and employers.

Of the former, my favorite came from a 2012 graduate of an elite Virginia college, who wrote me to say that "America has a hefty appetite for BS, and I'm ready and willing to deliver on that demand." I gave him points for boldness and cheekily wrote back asking if we might consider his letter for publication. The bravado vanished; he demurred.

Well, Class of 2012, I did you a (small) injustice. At least the pretense of knowledgeability was important to you. For the Class of 2014, it seems that inviolable ignorance is the only true bliss.

It's not just the burgeoning list of rescinded invitations to potentially offensive commencement speakers: Ayaan Hirsi Ali at Brandeis, Condi Rice at Rutgers, Christine Lagarde at Smith, and Robert Birgeneau at Haverford.

In February, students at Dartmouth issued a list of seventy-two demands for "transformative justice." Among them: "mandate sensitivity training"; "organize continuous external reviews of the College's structural racism, classism, ableism, sexism and heterosexism"; and "create a policy banning the Indian mascot." When the demands weren't automatically met, the students seized an administration building.

At Brown, a Facebook page is devoted to the subject of "Micro/Aggressions," a growth area in the grievance industry. Example of a microaggression: "As a dark-skinned Black person, I feel alienated from social justice spaces or conversations about institutional racism here at Brown when non-Black people of color say things like 'let's move away from the White-Black binary.'"

And then there are "trigger warnings." In Saturday's *New York Times*, Jennifer Medina reports that students and like-minded faculty are demanding warnings on study materials that trigger "symptoms of post-traumatic stress disorder." Chinua Achebe's *Things Fall Apart* was cited by one faculty document at Oberlin as a novel that could "trigger readers who have experienced racism, colonialism, religious persecution, violence, suicide and more."

Similar Tipper Gore–type efforts are under way at UC Santa Barbara, George Washington University, and other second- and third-tier schools. Did I just offend some readers by saying that? Sorry, but it's true. Any student who demands—and gets— emotional pampering from his university needs to pay a commensurate price in intellectual derision. College was once about preparing boys and girls to become men and women, not least through a process of desensitization to discomfiting ideas. Now it's just a $240,000 extension of kindergarten. Maybe Oberlin can start offering courses in Sharing Is Caring. Students can read *The Gruffalo* with trigger warnings that it potentially stigmatizes people with hairy backs.

This is the bind you find yourselves in, Class of 2014: no society, not even one that cossets the young as much as ours does, can treat you as children forever. A central teaching of Genesis is that knowledge is purchased at the expense of innocence. A core teaching of the ancients is that personal dignity is obtained through habituation to virtue. And at least one basic teaching of true liberalism is that the essential right of free people is the right to offend, and an essential responsibility of free people is to learn how to cope with being offended.

I'll grant you this: It's not all your fault. The semi- and postliterates who overran the humanities departments at most universities long before I ever set foot in college are the main culprits here. Then again, it shouldn't be that hard to figure out what it takes to live in a free country. The ideological brainwashing that takes place on campus isn't (yet) coercive. Mainly, it's just onanistic.

There's good news in that. You can still take charge of your education, and of your lives. The cocoon years are over; the microaggressions are about to pour down.

Do Your Best to
Be Your Best

★

CLARENCE THOMAS

University of Georgia

Class of 2008

JUSTICE CLARENCE THOMAS has been a justice of the U.S. Supreme Court since 1991. Here he addresses students in his home state of Georgia.

One of the sobering realizations that I came to while thinking about and preparing to be here today is that most of the graduates from the undergraduate program had not started the first grade when I went onto the Court. Life comes at you fast, and passes even faster.

In 1971, when I sat where you all are now sitting as graduates, I was just glad to be done with college. I was both scared and anxious about the rest of my life. My grandmother and mother were both there in the stadium bleachers to support me and to be there for my wedding the next day. Absent was the one person I wanted and needed there—my grandfather. Mired in a distracting mixture of fear, apprehension, and sadness, I wondered just what would happen next. How would I repay my student loans? Where would I live?

Somewhere through this fog of self-absorbed confusion, I barely noticed the graduation speaker. His name was Michael Harrington, the author of the then-popular book *The Other America: Poverty in the United States*, and himself a Holy Cross graduate. He seemed to be exhorting us on to solve the problems of poverty and injustice. As important as those are, I, like most people sitting there that day, was more focused on whether I would be able to solve my own problems, so that I would not become a problem for, or a burden to, others.

So having sat where you are sitting today, I have no illusion that I am at the center of your attention, nor do I think that what I have to say will be long remembered. But I do humbly request a few moments of your attention, recognizing that there is much going on in your lives. I promise that I will not clutter up your special day with my own ruminations about jurisprudence, although I do have an interest in discussing, at some point, my views on the Dormant Commerce Clause. [laughter] I take that as a lack of interest.

I will say in passing, however, that even today, after almost seventeen years on the Court, many of the lessons that I learned about life and academics still serve me well on the

Court and in life. Believe me, what you have learned thus far really matters and matters greatly.

I will also not bore you with another litany of complaints or grievances, or exhortations to solve the problems that none of us of advanced years have been able to solve, or in some cases, even understand. It seems to be standard fare these days to charge young people to go out and do great things. Often what is meant is that they do something "out there" as opposed to their personal lives. Many years ago, when I read Dickens's novel *Bleak House*, I was fascinated by Mrs. Jellyby's obsession with her telescopic philanthropy—her great projects in Africa—while at the same time her task at hand went undone. Realistically, the great battles for most of us involve conquering ourselves and discharging our duties at hand. These are the building blocks for the great things.

When I take stock of the nearly six decades of my life, the great people are mostly the people of my youth—my grandparents, my relatives, my neighbors, my teachers. One of the things they all had in common was the way they discharged their daily duties and their daily responsibilities—conscientiously and without complaint or grievance. I think of relatives like Cousin Hattie, who cleaned rooms at the Midway Hotel in Liberty County; her husband, Cousin Robert, who cut grass and farmed; and Miss Gertrude, who labored as a maid. They went about their lives, doing their best with what they had, knowing all the while that this was not necessarily fair. They played the hand they were dealt. And, through it all, they were unfailingly good, kind, and decent people whose unrequited love for our great country and hope for our future were shining examples for us to emulate in our own struggles.

Whether in the merciless summer heat of Liberty County or the sudden downpours at the bus stop at Henry and East Broad streets in Savannah, they taught us how to live with personal dignity and respect for one another. To this day, the people who do their jobs, raise their families, and sacrifice so that we can gather here in peace are my heroes, from whom I draw great inspiration.

Quite a lot has happened in my lifetime, as I alluded to earlier. Monumental events involving constitutional and civil rights have made it possible for me to stand here today, when I could not sit there years ago as a college graduate. There are also the technological advances: from the scrub board to the automatic washing machine; the dishwasher (that is one of my personal favorites); the television; the computer; the iPod; and of course the now omnipresent cell phone.

My wife, who is my best friend in the world, often comments on the range of my life. I have been blessed to know and befriend the best and the least educated, the wealthiest and the poorest, the healthy and the physically challenged. I have seen a lot in my journey from the black soil of South Georgia to the white marble of the Supreme Court. It has been a longer journey than the miles from there to Washington could ever suggest. Along the way, I have learned many lessons. There is a saying that if you want to know what is down the road, ask the person who is coming back.

Today I am coming back down the dusty and difficult road of my life to meet at the commencement of your journey, the beginning of your journey, through the rest of your lives. I would just like to take a few more minutes of your precious time here at the side of this road between the hedges. I have just a few modest suggestions; I promise I will not hold you up very long.

First, show gratitude and appreciation. None of you, not one of you, made it here entirely on your own. There are people in your lives who gave you birth, who raised you and loved you, even when you were not so lovable. Thank the people who put up with your antics and loved you through it all. Thank the people who paid your tuition and your expenses. There are those who helped and counseled you through difficult times or when you made hard decisions. There are those who were compassionate enough to tell you what you needed to hear, not what you wanted to hear. Take some time today to thank them.

Don't put it off; some of us did.

I never took the time to properly thank my grandparents, the two people who saved my life and made it possible for me to stand here today. Deep down, I know they understand, as they always did and as parents always seem to find a way to understand. But it is still a burden that I will carry to my grave. Take some time to thank those who helped you.

A simple thank-you will do wonders. You may never know how much that expression of gratitude will mean. Twenty-five years ago, I went to visit my eighth-grade teacher, Sister Mary Virgilius, for the first time since high school. I thanked her for all she had done for me and for being compassionate enough to tell me about my deficiencies when I was in the eighth grade. I told her that I assumed that after more than forty years of teaching, I was among a long list of students who had come back to thank her.

She said, "No, you're the first."

One additional word about her. On one of my recent visits to her at the retirement convent in New Jersey, she showed a friend and me her tiny room. It had a small bed, a bureau, and a chair. While telling us about her room, she listed the items to be given away after her death. She's almost ninety-five years old now. A rosary to her niece; a prayer book to the Franciscan sisters. There was a large photo of her and me on her bureau. Lovingly embracing it, she said, "This goes in my coffin with me."

Take a few minutes today to say thank you to anyone who helped you get here. Then try to live your lives as if you really appreciate their help and the good it has done in your lives. Earn the right to have been helped by the way you live your lives.

Next, remember that life is not easy for any of us. It will probably not be fair, and it certainly is not all about you. The gray hair and wrinkles you see on older people have been earned the hard way, by living and dealing with the challenges of life.

When I was a young adult and labored under the delusion of my own omniscience, I thought I knew more than I actually did. That is a function of youth.

With the wisdom that only comes with the passage of years, the older folks warned me presciently and ominously, "Son, you just live long enough and you'll see." They were right; oh, so right. Life is humbling and can be hard, very hard. It is a series of decisions, some harder than others, some good and, unfortunately, too many of them bad. It will be up to each of you to make as many good decisions as possible and to limit the bad ones, then to learn from all of them. But I will urge you to resist when those around you insist on making the bad decisions. Being accepted or popular with those doing wrong is an awful Faustian bargain and, as with all Faustian bargains, not worth it. It is never wrong to do the right thing. It may be hard, but never wrong.

Each of you is about to begin a new journey. Whatever that may be, do it well. If you are going to a new job or the military or to graduate school, do it to the best of your abilities. Each year at the Court I hire four new law clerks. They are the best of the best. The major difference between them and most of their classmates is self-discipline. By self-discipline, I mean doing what you are supposed to do and not doing what you aren't supposed to do.

Though there are many enticements and distractions, it is up to each of you to take care of your respective business. Remember, the rewards of self-indulgence are not nearly as great as the rewards of self-discipline.

But even as you take care of business, there are a few other necessities for the journey. At the very top of the list are the three F's—faith, family, and friends. When all else fails and we feel like prodigal sons and daughters, they will always be there, even if we don't deserve them. Having needed them, I know they will always be your saving grace.

Trustworthiness and honesty are next. If you can't be trusted with small matters, how can you be trusted with important ones? It may be hard to be honest, but it is never wrong. For my part, I can only work with honest people. I need to be able to trust them, and so will you.

Conscientiousness and timeliness are invaluable habits and character traits. As I tell my law clerks, I want my work done right and I want it on time. No matter what you do, do it right and do it on time. My brother used to say that he hurried up to be early so he could wait. Not a bad idea.

Stay positive. There will be many around you who are cynical and negative. These cause cancers of the spirit and they add nothing worthwhile. Don't inhale their secondhand cynicism and negativism. Some, even those with the most opportunities in this, the greatest country, will complain and grieve ceaselessly, ad infinitum and ad absurdum. It may be fair to ask them, as they complain about the lack of perfection in others and our imperfect institutions, just what they themselves are perfect at.

Look, many have been angry at me because I refuse to be angry, bitter, or full of grievances, and some will be angry at you for not becoming agents in their most recent cynical causes. Don't worry about it. No monuments are ever built to cynics. Associate with people who add to your lives, not subtract; people you are comfortable introducing to the best people in your lives—your parents, your family, your friends, your mentors, your ministers.

Always have good manners. This is a time-honored tradition and trait; it is not old-fashioned. Good manners will open doors that nothing else will. And given the choice between two competent persons, most of us will opt to hire the one with good manners. For example, no matter what older adults say about calling them by their first names, don't. Believe me, they remember, and not as kindly as you might think. I thank God my grandparents made me put a handle on grown folks' names and taught me to say "please" and "thank you."

Finally, the Golden Rule that is virtually universal—treat

others the way you want to be treated. Indeed, when others hurt you, you may well be required to treat them far better than they treated you and far better than human nature would suggest they deserve. Be better than they are.

Help others as you wanted and needed to be helped. If you want to receive kindness, respect, and compassion, you must first give them. But to do that, you must first have them yourselves to give. Almost thirty years ago, a janitor in the U.S. Senate with whom I often spoke pulled me aside. I must have looked like the weight of the world was on my shoulders; at the very least, I must have looked despondent, not an uncommon look for a young man with common difficulties and hoping to make some difference in the lives of others. In sober, measured, and nearly toothless diction, he counseled me, "Son, you cannot give what you do not have." He was right, and merely echoed what I had heard throughout my youth in South Georgia.

My grandfather would look at the fields late in the summer and make the point that we could not give to others if we had not worked all summer to plant, till, and harvest. As a child, that meant little; as a man, I know he was right.

There are no guarantees in life, but even with all its uncertainties and challenges it is worth living the right way. As you commence the next chapter in your young lives, I urge you to do your best to be your best. Each of you is a precious building block for your families, your university, your communities, and our great country. It is truly up to each of you to decide exactly what kind of building block you will be.

Gridlock, an American Achievement

GEORGE F. WILL

Niagara University

Class of 2014

GEORGE F. WILL is a Pulitzer Prize–winning syndicated columnist and network television commentator. He worked for many years at ABC-TV. He is now a FOX News contributor.

I am, I should confess, a lapsed professor. I grew up a faculty brat—my father was a professor of philosophy at the University of Illinois and I began my life after college as a professor.

I am, you will be happy to know, aware that I should not detain you for long. I am, after all, the last person standing between you and the wider world. It is about a small portion of that world about which I wish to speak. It is the world of politics.

I want to take this occasion to thank you, who are today graduating, for all the hours, days, weeks—months, actually—that you are going to work to support me and others who are, or soon will be, as I am, elderly. You see, the primary business of today's government—of our welfare state or entitlement state; call it what you will—is to transfer wealth from the working young and middle aged to the retired elderly, in the form of pensions and health care: Social Security and Medicare.

This is a regressive transfer of wealth, because the elderly are, after a lifetime of accumulation, more affluent than the population is generally. And because the welfare state is especially important to the elderly, the elderly are especially apt to vote. Hence we increasingly have the politics of gerontocracy—government by, as well as for, the elderly.

So, again, I say: thank you in advance for all that you are going to spend, through taxes on my behalf.

Now, if you, during your family-forming and house-buying years, would rather not spend quite so much of your time and your earnings supporting people like me, you are going to have to pay attention to politics—particularly, to Washington.

For four-and-a-half decades I have lived there, participating in our great public controversies. Washington has been described as an enclave surrounded on four sides by reality. But Washington, too, is reality.

Indeed, it is time to take seriously the truth that we do indeed have a representative government. It really does represent the realities of the American mind, with all that mind's conflicts.

So, if we are embarrassed by Washington, we should be embarrassed about ourselves.

I think every public speaker should have a clear point to make. My model of such a speaker is the late Conrad Hilton, the hotel tycoon. In one national television appearance he was invited to tell the national audience the one thing, based on his life's experience, he would most like his listeners to hear. Hilton turned to the camera, looked America in the eye, and said: "Please—put the curtain inside the tub."

His message may have lacked metaphysical profundity but it was nicely practical. So is my message, which is this:

There is much talk today about the heated discord in Washington. The discord is real enough, but the bigger problem is a consensus. The consensus is as broad as the Republic and as deep as the Grand Canyon. This consensus is that we should have a large, generous welfare state—and not pay for it.

Rather, we should borrow a significant portion of the cost of our consumption of government goods and services. This places the burden of paying for this portion on the unconsenting, because unborn, members of future generations.

We should not sugarcoat this practice. It is a decadent democracy. We used to run deficits—we used to borrow—for the future. We won wars and built roads and bridges and dams and airports for the future. Now we are borrowing from the future, to pay for our own comforts.

If you would want to help change this, and I hope you do, you are going to have to participate in politics. But if you do, you are going to have to understand the patience required by the American political system.

Nowadays it is constantly said that Washington is dysfunctional because it is so difficult to get things done there. My message to you is: it is supposed to be difficult.

It is constantly said that Washington's worst aspect is gridlock. My message to you is that gridlock is not an American problem, it is an American achievement.

Here is why. When the Constitution's framers assembled in Philadelphia in the sweltering summer of 1787, they did not set out to produce an efficient government. Rather, they wanted to create a safe government. A government strong enough to protect our natural rights, but not so strong that it could threaten them.

The most important word in our nation's most important document, the Declaration of Independence, is the word "secure." The Declaration says: We hold it to be self-evident that all persons are created equal, and endowed by their creator with inalienable rights. And governments are instituted to secure those rights.

Note well: government exists not to give us our rights but to secure our rights that preexist government.

To make government safe, the Framers filled our government with blocking mechanisms designed to make it difficult to move. The Framers framed three independent and rival branches of government. And two rival branches of the legislative branch. The Framers created supermajority requirements. And presidential vetoes. And legislative veto overrides. And judicial review.

Passage of legislation was made deliberately difficult. You need not just one majority but concurrent majorities. A majority in the House of Representatives, with its unique constituencies and electoral rhythms. And a majority in the Senate, with its different constituencies and electoral rhythms.

Does this take time? Yes. Is it difficult? Certainly. But it is supposed to be difficult. Our system is designed to protect us from majorities that are turbulent, transient, and dangerous.

That is, our constitutional system is designed to protect us from ourselves—from our tumultuous passions and our imprudent desires.

There are strong passions now roiling our politics. But there is a good reason why the temperature of American politics is unusually high today.

This is because the stakes are unusually high. We are debating about two fundamental values of Western political philosophy—freedom and equality. These are both important; they are always somewhat in tension; the tension is constantly being adjusted.

Today, liberals emphasize equality—not just equal opportunity but increased equality of social outcomes. Hence they advocate the expansion of entitlement programs that make more and more Americans equally dependent on a common source of material well-being, the government.

Conservatives today emphasize freedom more than equality. Hence they prefer market forces rather than government to allocate wealth and opportunity. And they regard the multiplication of entitlement programs as inimical to the public good because they regard them as subversive of the attitudes and aptitudes essential for a free society, such as thrift, industrious-ness, self-reliance, and deferral of gratifications.

Now, there are empirical questions at issue in today's sharp disagreements between liberals and conservatives. Questions such as: What are the behavioral effects of entitlement pro-grams? And: Do markets efficiently and fairly allocate wealth and opportunity?

Furthermore, there are many honorable and intelligent men and women passionately engaged on both sides of this debate. Their passions are proportional to the stakes of the argument.

And I hope you will join them. After all, you, members of the Class of 2014, are today certified as having met the high standards of a university that is a custodian of a great tradition in Western philosophy, including political philosophy. Catholic thinkers, from Augustine to Aquinas to Cardinal Newman to Pope John Paul II, have produced some of the most profound reflections on the right kind of regime to facilitate human flourishing.

And speaking of human flourishing, I would be remiss if I concluded my remarks without offering a tribute to one of the noblest aspects of this noble university.

Niagara University is a pioneering national leader in help-ing the developmentally disabled participate in our society. This matters to me.

My son Jon has Down syndrome, a congenital genetic disabil-ity that involves, among other things, varying degrees of mental retardation. When Jon was born, a hospital official asked his mother and me if we intended to take Jon home. We said yes, we thought that was what people did with their newborn children.

This was in 1972. Times, and attitudes, have changed for the better, thanks in part to institutions like Niagara University.

When Jon was born, the life expectancy of persons with Down syndrome was about twenty. Last Sunday, Jon celebrated his forty-second birthday. Our Down syndrome citizens are living longer, and flourishing, because America has become more welcoming to them, helping them learn and work.

Jon works in the Washington Nationals clubhouse. He gets up every morning and goes to work at a major league ballpark. Which means he has a better job than I have.

So I want to thank Niagara University not only for allowing me the pleasure of your company today, but also for helping so many people like Jon. And I want to emphasize the message of Jon's life: Change is possible. Change can be dramatic. And change begins when places like Niagara University decide that there is a moral imperative for change.

Now, Class of 2014, go forth and make this great university as proud of you as you have a right to be of the diplomas you have earned here.

Surprise Yourself

★

JUAN WILLIAMS

Whitman College

May 2010

JUAN WILLIAMS is a former columnist for *The Washington Post* and an award-winning author. He became a commentator on FOX News after being fired by National Public Radio for voicing opinions deemed to be politically incorrect.

Change is all around us and in this uncertain environment, so, too, is anxiety. Today's graduates are going into a tough job market—competition for graduate study as well as jobs, for internships, even volunteer positions is high. Trust in American leadership—positions that you will occupy as people look to you with your Whitman education—trust in leadership is at an all-time low from Washington, to the Vatican, to Wall Street. Most Americans tell pollsters they think the country is headed in the wrong direction. At this moment of great anxiety and un-certainty, let me remind you, today's graduates, that you are the best—you are good people with good education and, as you can see by all of us gathered here, you are much loved. You are the chosen children. You've met expectations of your parents, your teachers, your coaches. This is no time to begin acting out of fear, anger, and finger-pointing. This is no time for retrenching in terms of your plans or changing plans to somehow take into account this very tough moment. In fact, if you want to make God laugh, let me suggest that you tell her your plans.

This is a moment to go beyond expectations, to reach inside and do the unexpected. Surprise your parents. Surprise your teachers. Surprise your friends (they never thought you'd get here anyway). But most of all, surprise yourself. Go beyond what makes you comfortable. Open yourself to ideas, events, relation-ships that make you uncomfortable. Travel places where you know no one. Learn another language. Create art, even though you're not an artist. Argue with people. Fall down. Get up. Read books, all sorts of books. Mark Twain once said: "A man who does not read has no advantage over a man who can't read."

So read. Be curious. Understand, as Whitman has taught you, as these faculty have sought to ingrain in you, that true free-dom is the freedom to avoid manipulation by fear; that true free-dom is being able to avoid the evil that comes from not thinking; that true freedom is the ability to avoid the evil that comes from not caring, not excelling, and not believing that you can do it.

Think back to those great-grandparents and grandparents who overcame the Depression, World War II, Korea, Vietnam, the Cold War. Think of the limits that existed fifty years ago for women, Blacks, and immigrants in this country. I would ask you to surprise yourself.

As a journalist, I have the opportunity to meet all sorts of world leaders. And I can't tell you how often this comes to me— that these people are surprising themselves every day: that that is their distinguishing characteristic. I remember meeting Nelson Mandela after he had just come out of jail. I was in his home in Soweto, South Africa. It was an odd moment in that there were so many journalists from all around the world there wanting a moment of Mandela's time. But it turned out I had written a book about the American civil rights movement that he had read while he was in jail. In fact, he's one of the few people I've ever met who read the book before he saw the TV series.

When he saw my name on a list of people who wanted to greet him on his release, he said, "Well, I'd like to meet the author," and I was put in a line with ambassadors and the like to shake hands with Nelson Mandela. Well, once I got up there, I wouldn't let go of his hand. And I said: "Please, Mr. Mandela, I come from Washington, D.C., in the United States of America. It would mean so much to us to just have a moment of your time for an interview. Please, please, please." Of course at this point his aides—you know how it looks when you have a bad comedian on the stage and they give him the hook?—his aides are pulling me to get me out of there, so I finally let go of his hand. But just when I'm about to hit the door, he says, "Well, you're a writer and I have some personal correspondence I need to take care of, and if you're willing to help me, you can stay around and I'll talk to you when I can." I said, "That's a deal, I'll do it!" So I ended up writing silly letters, things like "Thank You Comrade Gorbachev. It's great to be out. See you soon, love Nelson." Yeah, you guys laugh, but I got my interview, I tell you that!

So, I'm doing this stuff, and then, of course, I'm seeing Mandela as he's having meals with his children, seeing old friends, relatives, really an unbelievable moment, and at one point everybody gets up from the table, and I say to him: "Mr. Mandela, from the time that you were a child, you must have had a desire to break apart this cruel apartheid system, to take on the racism in this society."

This very serious man begins to laugh out loud. And I think, "Oh my God, there must have been some cultural miscommunication. He didn't get it." But he says, "No, no, no." He says, "No, everybody says this to me." He says when he was a young man, the only thing he wanted to rebel against were his parents! He said he wanted to move away from them, he thought they were stuck in the mud, they didn't know what was going on. Remember, this is a guy who would have been a prince had he just stayed. He was attracted to the lights of the bright city: He wanted to go to Johannesburg. He wanted to see what life was like. He wanted to become a boxer. His parents couldn't understand it. Then he wanted to learn the language of the Dutch settlers. And his friends couldn't understand. And then he wanted what he called a Western-style education. . . .

Then he said he wanted to go to law school, and even his closest friends said, "You know Nelson, a black man, a black lawyer in South Africa, you're not going to have any juice. No one's going to hire you. This is a hard life. Why would you do this?" He went to law school.

Then he got out of law school, and he was representing the few clients that were attracted to him as a young black man. He found that he was frustrated by dealing with the legal system, that the courts did not honor their rights, did not listen to his arguments. So he got involved with political activists, with the African National Congress, and pretty soon they had him giving a few speeches, and wouldn't you know it, the government identified Mandela as a leader, and pretty soon he was in the dock, and pretty soon he was confined to Robben Island. And you couldn't wear a T-shirt with his picture on it. Journalists couldn't type his name in the newspaper. You couldn't hear a Mandela speech on the radio. It was all illegal. He was viewed as that powerful. And, of course, when he was released from prison, well, his light had shone beyond the borders of South Africa. Now he was a beacon, a beacon of the freedom movement to the world, and you had journalists, including me, coming from around the world to simply get a glimpse of him, to hear what he had to say.

I think to myself as I look out at all of you today that right here are future Nelson Mandelas. Right here are people who don't know where life's road is taking them. Today among you are people who are going to make history, but maybe even more so people who are going to make a difference. Because you are a light to the world, you are our greatest hope. You are educated. You are loved. And that's why I would ask that you make your highest priority on this day to surprise yourself. To allow your imagination to run wild. To test your ability to surprise yourself, challenge yourself in every way. . . .

The Art of the Entrepreneur

MORTIMER ZUCKERMAN

Berkeley College

MORTIMER ZUCKERMAN is the founding
chairman of Boston Properties, the publisher of the New
York *Daily News*, and the editor in chief of *U.S. News &
World Report*.

Ceremonies such as commencements are always special in
the eyes of anyone who has had a chance to participate in them. I
speak to you at a remarkable time when you enter the world and
an economy that is in the midst of an extraordinary transformation of distribution of goods, services, and knowledge, through
the Internet. The rush to create the hardware and software to expand the reach of the Internet has the capacity to power the world
in which you will work even further. Information industries have

now become the biggest job creators, and America has taken the lead in the highest value-added industries of microelectronics, computers, software, genetics, microbiology, et cetera.

These American achievements grew out of a culture that has long valued individualism, entrepreneurialism, pragmatism, and novelty—a direct descendant of the idea of the American frontier that has made Americans comfortable with change and celebrates mavericks and people who make things happen. This legacy has outlived the passing of the frontier and still inspires millions. American culture welcomes newcomers and immigrants and is dramatically open to energy and talent rising from the bottom up.

Flexibility, creativity, and optimism come naturally to an immigrant society, where the new is better than the old, where taking charge is valued over playing safe, where making money is superior to inheriting it, and where education is favored over family ties. We foster the upstart, the rebel, the young, and the innovator, and nourish and reward the nimble new firms, which make up the most versatile economic unit, and whose innovations have been critical to the resurgence of our economy.

Entrepreneurialism and individual initiative have been so widely accepted that in every recent decade roughly two million new businesses have been started. Smaller companies have demonstrated their capacity to compete in this swiftly changing environment with flexibility, rapid response, openness, innovation, and the ability to attract the best people.

The American economy is thus suited for today's rapidly changing, knowledge-based economy, even more than it was for the mass production industrial economy of earlier days. The new bottom-up economic environment is tantamount to a giant information processing system that has an enhanced capacity to absorb, adapt to, and manage ongoing revolutions in technology, information, and logistics, that are too dynamic and complex to be handled by any top-down system, no matter how talented its bureaucracy, government, or corporate leadership.

The marriage of the new economy and an older American culture is a happy one. This energy has been matched by a transformation of the world of finance capital that has proven its capacity to provide the entrepreneurial capital needed by entrepreneurial management, willing to provide the money to back new ideas. That is why America is the only country that funds so many of its young, who are the most comfortable and creative with the new technologies, and why America's capital increasingly funds the future, not the past, the new and not the old. So as the poet Ovid once wrote, "I am happy not to be born in ancient times. I am glad to be born in these." And so should you.

I would like to spend a few moments talking to you about the particular kind of character that you have undoubtedly read much about. He, or she, is properly known today as the entrepreneur, who is really sort of an artist, in a sense that artists create things—and also is a revolutionary, in the sense that when he, or she, gets involved with something, it is presumably not the same as before.

The entrepreneur is more often than not an individual, someone with whom we can all identify ourselves a little more easily than with, say, a large corporation. There is more than just a cultural affinity for the entrepreneur that makes us pay attention to this particular character. It is also the fact that most of the new jobs in this economy are being created in companies that employ under twenty people, and 80 percent of the new jobs have been created in companies that employ under a hundred people. Why? Because fifty years ago, we needed mass-produced goods to meet most of our particular needs. We tended to be associated with large companies, with large concentrations of labor, and physical and capital resources. But as our affluence has grown, as our population has become more educated, and our wants have multiplied and become less material, more fragmented, more individualistic, there is less need for mass-produced goods and more need for individually designed products.

These tend to come from smaller businesses, especially in the high-tech area. Indeed, the history of recent high-tech developments is almost exclusively a study of individuals who took great risks and endured considerable hardship to develop and market their ideas.

Now, it wouldn't be appropriate to discuss an entrepreneur without discussing the psychology of the entrepreneur—certainly in an age of analysis. To understand the entrepreneur, as an old teacher of mine, Professor Abraham Zaleznik of the Harvard Business School, used to say—in terms that I could personally understand—"You first have to understand the psychology of the juvenile delinquent." The hallmark of the entrepreneur is a drive for autonomy, for freedom from restraint that speaks of an inner rebelliousness and fearlessness in the face of risk—as well as optimism.

This reminds me of the story of the difference between the optimist and the pessimist. The optimist thinks this is the best of all possible worlds—and the pessimist fears he may be right.

But an entrepreneur is an optimist because he is sure that he cannot fail. No matter how many times he may fail, he will still believe in the successful outcome of his next effort. Psychoanalysts who have studied entrepreneurs say that lurking within these supremely self-confident businesspeople, in many cases, is a small child who is striving to create in the business world the world that he craved in his childhood—a world with him, or her, as the star outrivaling his father. The force that propelled the entrepreneur into his solitary orbit is a craving for autonomy.

The entrepreneur must not only be a brilliant creator, he must also often have to be able to build the team and recruit those who offer the skills he lacks. And so he must inspire others with his vision and drive.

A constant characteristic of the entrepreneur is charisma, a social adroitness spiced with a winning kind of evangelism, the ability to persuade people to believe in something that has never been done before and also involves planning without clear goals, not only to be comfortable in setting out without knowing exactly how he is going to get there or even where there is, but to have a sense of creating confidence that he will get there, in part developing confidence in his intuition—for successful entrepreneurs thrive on hunches, speculation, and a gut sense, and, of course, the ability to take risks. An entrepreneur gravitates to risk while others shy away from perils.

The successful ones also learn how to be wily and risk-taking, so the gamble is less large than it would be for someone else, and he believes in himself so much that he calculates the odds differently.

Of course the entrepreneur generally does not have the staying power of the manager. He may be suited to build the company but is often less suited to run it—sort of like a sprinter forced to run a marathon.

But there is a dark side: the rather insatiable need for applause and to be noticed, that psychologists say grows out of a deep-seated fear of being insignificant. The danger, of course, is that some people do things just to be noticed when it makes no particular sense.

In other words, being an entrepreneur is an enormously satisfying role, as you try to do something that almost has never been done before, despite the natural resistance in the outside world to novelty and new ideas.

These days there has been an enormous revival of interest in the entrepreneur and the entrepreneurial function. Why? Because we have entered a New World of global competition and seek out areas where we have a comparative advantage.

But there is one more question I would like to ask. If we want this entrepreneurship, this inventiveness and risk taking, how do we go about doing it?

Well, one, is not to overwhelm them with government, an institution which may do anything but surely cannot pick winners. Entrepreneurs cannot be programmed. But they do have perseverance.

Do not be discouraged. In 1865, *The Boston Post* wrote about

Alexander Graham Bell's attempt to develop the telephone that "well-informed people not only believe it is impossible to transmit voices over wires but that, were it possible to do so, this would be of no practical value." Thomas Edison himself said in 1880 that the phonograph "would not be of any commercial value" and that "when the Paris exhibition," where the electric light was being shown, "closes the electric light will close with it." Thomas Watson, the IBM chairman, said in 1943, "I think there is a world market for about five computers." And remember Thomas Malthus, the British economist, who predicted in 1798 that the imbalance between population growth and food production would cause the world to starve to death. The doomsayers called it the Malthusian Iron Law. It was neither iron nor law. Malthus fell into the oldest trap in the prognostication game, he underestimated everyone's intelligence but his own. He was incapable of seeing that out of the industrial revolution would come reapers, threshers, combines, and tractors, and thus did not foresee the quantum jump in the productivity of food, to the point where we now have such an abundance that foolish governments today pay farmers not to cultivate the soil at all.

So let's not allow the experts to tell us what to do and what not to do, or to place restrictions on the freedoms you may need to develop your interests, your inventions, or your innovations.

But risk is not synonymous with recklessness. There is a business theory of risk management, which was inspired by the following: "It is only when the tide goes out that you see who has been swimming without a bathing suit." But, if there is one more thing that I want to convey to you it is that it is impossible to provide formulas to solve the problems you face. But remember that nothing in the world can take the place of persistence. Talent will not—nothing is more common than unsuccessful men with talent. Genius will not—unrewarded genius is almost a cliché. Education will not—the world is full of educated derelicts. It is persistence and determination in combination with talent and education that will see you through and that has solved and will solve the problems of our country and the world.

Or to put it another way, the definition of genius is lasting five minutes longer than the other side. I wish all of you many five minutes in your career.

ACKNOWLEDGMENTS

I want to thank Sentinel's Adrian Zackheim for his enthusiastic embrace of this project; Bria Sandford for her keen editorial judgment; and Jesse Maeshiro for her tireless efforts to get this ready to go.

I am grateful to all the brilliant contributors to this anthology. It was inspiring to spend time with their commencement speeches.

Thanks to Michal Chafets for reminding me (sweetly) that authorial brevity is a virtue.

Special thanks to my collaborator, Coby Beyer-Chafets. Very simply, I couldn't have done this without him.